Two Trips in Search of the Buddha

BY

Albert Shansky

authorHOUSE®

AuthorHouse™
1663 Liberty Drive, Suite 200
Bloomington, IN 47403
www.authorhouse.com
Phone: 1-800-839-8640

First published by AuthorHouse 12/1/2008

ISBN: 978-1-4389-2175-4 (sc)

Printed in the United States of America
Bloomington, Indiana

This book is printed on acid-free paper.

TWO TRIPS IN SEARCH OF THE BUDDHA

BY ALBERT SHANSKY

INTRODUCTION

Before you read the Two Trips in Search of the Buddha, I should like to introduce me. I was born on March 26, 1925 in Sheepshead Bay in Brooklyn, New York to a Jewish working class family. I had two older brothers and now only have a younger sister. I never knew my father who died when I was four years old. We were a poor family, but as my mother used to say, "It's no disgrace to be poor, it's just inconvenient."

The meaning of life for me became clear and patent when I was about eight years old. The year 1933 was the height of the Great Depression. I quickly learned the value of work, the ways of survival and the usefulness of self-reliance and independence. A growing consciousness of social inequity was developing during my adolescence until the age of fourteen when the Spanish Civil War ended and World War II began in 1939.

At the age of eighteen, shortly after graduation from Boys High School, I was drafted into the United States Army where I earned two battle stars, Rhineland and Northern France, in the European Theater of Operations. Upon being mustered out of army service in 1946, I immediately took up my college career at Brooklyn College where I graduated with a B.S. and an M.S. degree in chemistry. I then went on in 1951 to Illinois Institute of Technology in Chicago to earn a Ph.D. in biochemistry.

I worked as a chemist for various firms for more than fifty years, thirty years of which I was an independent consultant operating my own laboratory. During my chemical career I wrote and published more than sixty scientific papers and produced eighteen patents.

In 1947 I married Pearl Brody and as of this writing we have been married more than sixty years. We have four children who have produced seven grandchildren.

I spent three four-month summers from May until September in 1992, 1993, and 1994 learning and practicing Zen teachings at the Hosshinji Monastery in Obama, Japan. I also was a Zen practitioner at the Eiheiji Monastery in Fukui, Japan in 2006. I practice zazen (Zen meditation) every morning without fail, regardless of location. In addition, I pursued Shambhala training at the Naropa University in Boulder, Colorado, and completed a one-day intensive course on Islam at the Hartford Seminary in Hartford, Connecticut.

I have had a life-long love for scholarship and in 1978, at the age of fifty-three, I returned to college. I attended Fairfield University where I took a total of fifty-three courses, half in philosophy and half in art history over a twenty-year period. In 1995 I established a second career by accepting the position of Executive Vice President of the International Institute for Field-Being at Fairfield University on a part time basis while still pursuing my chemical consulting practice. As of this writing I have written and presented more than twelve papers on philosophy at various professional and scholarly organizations and conferences. I have written a book on Buddhism in thirteenth century Japan, titled The Extinction of Illusion, published by PublishAmerica, Frederick, MD, in March 2006. A second book was published March 2007 by PublishAmerica, Frederick, MD, on thirteenth century Japan and the beginning of Jodo Shinshu Buddhism, titled Shinran and Eshinni. In addition I have written a memoir titled, An American's Journey into Buddhism, published by McFarland & Company in 2008.

I have some experience as a pedagogue having taught biology at the Norwalk Community College and Analytical Chemistry at the Norwalk Technical Institute in the 1960s. In addition I have lectured to the history class, Pacific Rim, at Norwalk Community College on basic Buddhism in East Asia. And have lectured twice to the Asian history class at Fairfield University on Buddhism and Ukiyo-e woodblock prints respectively. I was appointed an adjunct professor and teach two three-credit courses, World Religions and Non-Western Philosophy, at Norwalk Community College. I am preparing to teach a three-credit course on Introduction to Philosophy in the fall of 2008 and possibly a course on Buddhism and Zen the following spring.

Now that you know all about me let me tell you how I first became interested in Buddhism. I made my first trip to Japan in 1968 and over the next forty years returned to Japan twenty times. That comes to about a trip to Japan every two years. These trips were mostly tourist trips but about a third was for business reasons. I was a chemical consultant to the Shiseido Research Laboratories in Yokohama and Bristol Myers Corporation in Tokyo. I have visited all four major islands of Japan – Hokkaido, Honshu, Kyushu, and Shikoku. In my travels I have not only stayed in the comfort of hotels but also have resided in ryokans and temples and monasteries. I speak Japanese haltingly but I know enough to get around with facility.

Ever since my first visit I was fascinated by Japanese culture. I admire their penchant for bowing, which is a form of respect expressed when meeting someone. They engage in cleanliness, particularly daily bathing almost as a ritualistic exercise, indeed, the Japanese word for beautiful (*kirei*) is the same word for clean. Their lifestyle and culture has been influenced over past centuries by their neighbors, particularly, China and Korea from whence they received Buddhism as a religion in the sixth century BCE and placed it in juxtaposition with Shinto their indigenous religion. This relationship is so cohesive that it is said, "Married in Shinto, buried in Buddhism." Most Japanese people are members of both religions.

As a tourist I began exploring museums and temples, where I viewed some of the most beautiful and spectacular art work of the Japanese religions. I became intrigued by Ukiyo-e woodblock prints and Japanese calligraphy and started collecting prints and scrolls. I am fond of watching Kabuki and Noh performances even though I require a "libretto" to fully enjoy them. But that's not all. I found that the Japanese enjoy Western music and Western drama as well as their native and esoteric art forms. I admit that I attended many of those performances as well.

When I looked at some of the Buddhist art work in temples and museums I had a grippingly need to learn more about what I was viewing. I had an eagerness to begin reading about Buddhism. I consumed many books on this subject so it did not take me long to find answers to my questions. In the early 1980s I found myself traveling to Minneapolis on business almost monthly. One day, as a lark, I attended Buddhist services at the Minnesota Zen Meditation Center on Lake Calhoun. The abbot of the Zen Center was Katagiri Roshi. who was sick at the time with terminal cancer. Prior to his demise he advised me to go to the Hosshinji Monastery in Obama, Japan, which was a training monastery for Zen monks. It was there, he said, I would learn about Buddhism and Buddhist monastic life. I wish I could have explained to Katagiri Roshi that I would first make these two trips to Japan in search of Buddhist ethic and Buddhist knowledge by meeting people on my travels. Unfortunately he died before I could speak with him. I remember, he always said, "You must train, practice, and live like a Zen monk."

I feel strongly that the two trips to Japan which I call, The Sea of Tranquility and The Divine Walk were important preliminary components of my life of practicing Buddhism. These two trips led me into a lifelong quest for Buddhist knowledge. As a result Buddhist enlightenment was acquired by intellectual and aesthetic practice.

Albert Shansky
Norwalk, Connecticut

THE FIRST TRIP

THE SEA OF TRANQUILITY

A JOURNEY THROUGH THE INLAND SEA OF JAPAN

DEDICATION

To Erika, Elizabeth, Jacqueline, Benjamin, Hanna, Micaela, Daniel and their parents and especially their grandmother Pearl who made it all possible.

PREFACE

This first trip, The Sea of Tranquility, is the first of two trips which describes my travels in Japan in search of the Buddhist ethic. The two trips in the series in chronological order is as follows:

1. The Sea of Tranquility (Travels through the Inland Sea of Japan in 1981)

2. The Divine Walk (Walking the Henro Pilgrimage of Shikoku in 1991)

The above two trips are travel memoirs which describe my incipient interest in Buddhism and show an earnest and detailed observation of Japanese culture and lifestyle.

The above two trips are factual novella; they complete the description of the great Buddhist concepts and ways of religious practice as evidenced in everyday Japanese life. Although these two trips can be read individually they do represent a continuous search for the Buddhist ethic. The idea of this book is to give an account of myself in the search for the meaning of the Buddhist ethic. The excerpts given here are from my encounters with people who understand the basic scriptures and major writings of Buddhist thinkers. For the most part these are people recognized by Buddhists themselves as representing the mainstream of Buddhist thought and practice. There is, of course, an enormous diversity within Buddhism and no fixed standard of orthodoxy. Nevertheless, even differing conceptions of the authentic tradition – and each school has some notion of orthodoxy – reveal a common ground of discussion. This is what I am trying to present in this book.

Buddhism has established a greater universality than any other religion in South and East Asia. This is the reason for my search in Japan. For the reader making a first approach to Buddhism it will be most useful to follow me in areas where the sense of the tradition is strong. For this purpose the line of development from the first trip to the second trip may provide a relatively coherent picture.

THE SEA OF TRANQUILITY

A JOURNEY THROUGH THE INLAND SEA OF JAPAN

BY ALBERT SHANSKY

I

The landscape kept running by as I looked out of the window of the "bullet train" (shinkansen). We were soaring like a bird through the countryside of the Kansai district, on the five- hour trip from Tokyo to Hiroshima. The train was following the ancient *Tokaido* road made famous in Japanese history as the "golden route" between the two main cities, Kyoto and Tokyo (formerly Edo). As I looked out the window I dreamily remembered how I got here.

After a week long consulting session with my client, Bristol-Myers Company in Tokyo I felt I needed a rest and so was advised by my contact person, Joe Takata that a wonderful vacation would be a boat trip through the emerald green Inland Sea known as *Seto Naikai.* Its beautiful tranquil waters are studded with tiny pine covered islands. And its numerous diminutive fishing boats offer views of a Japan barely touched by modernity. There are more than three thousand islands in the Inland Sea, and I expect to visit only a fragment of them while plying back and forth between the two coastlines of Honshu and Shikoku.

The Inland Sea covers an area of nearly four million acres, is 260 miles long and varying in width from two-and-a-half to forty miles. It lies in the shelter of three of Japan's four main islands – Honshu, Kyushu, and Shikoku. Of the 3000 islands that it contains, some of them are more than 100 miles in circumference and others are mere dots of green that lie like a mirage on the blue and sparkling waters of the sea.

The area bounded by the Inland Sea represents the true Japan – the Japan of ancient customs, crafts, and superlative scenery. Its waters teem with fish, and the land blossoms with orchards, vegetable plantations, and tiers of paddy fields that rise like giant staircases up the sides of the hilly slopes that flank the shores of the sea.

I was brought out of my reverie by a vendor wheeling a cart down the aisle of the train shouting *EKI-BEN, EKI-BEN* (train station lunch). I was getting hungry and decided to buy a *bento* (lunch box) and a container of cold tea. The bento contained rice and cooked fish with vegetables; all served cold. After eating a satisfactory meal I thought about my first stop, Hiroshima. Our train went through the mountains and along the shore of the Inland Sea and after a five-hour journey we came to Shin Hiroshima (Hiroshima station).

The most striking thing about the city is the way in which it has been rebuilt. Most of the buildings have been put up since 1955. It gives the impression of being a thoroughly modern and progressive city. I had arranged to stay at the Hotel Hiroshima Grand on Kami Hatcho Bori Street.

Staying near the center of the city, I was able to hear the peals of bells from the Peace Memorial Hall, which ring twice a day, and those in the Roman Catholic Cathedral, all of which were gifts from abroad. The Peace Memorial Park contains a cenotaph and a marble tomb in which are lists of the names of known atomic bomb victims. Through the cenotaph I was able to see the ruins of the Industrial Exhibition Hall, whose dome is preserved as a symbol of the bombed city.

For me this was a very emotional experience. I am a veteran of World War II and was on duty in the European Theater when the atomic bomb was dropped on Hiroshima. I little understood the devastation it created until I read books and other accounts about the after effects. However, being here at this time (1981) brought it all back in a most meaningful way.

After a day of touring the city I returned to the hotel for rest and sustenance. At the front desk where I retrieved my room key the desk clerk told me that a man was waiting for me in the lobby. How could this be? I was not known to anyone in Hiroshima. The front desk clerk pointed to a young gentleman sitting in one of the wicker chairs. As I approached him, to my astonishment, I realized that the man was absolutely beautiful. Pale and elegantly reserved, with ringlets of honey-colored hair, a straight sloping nose, a lovely mouth, almond shaped eyes, and an expression of divinely blessed solemnity. His face called to mind the best product of an East-West marriage.

He sat in semi profile across from my point of observation, one patent-leather-clad foot before the other. His elbow propped on the armrest of the wicker chair, cheek glued to a closed hand. It was a posture of relaxed dignity. Who was he? What did he want?

"Konnichiwa, watakushi namae Shansky Albert." (Hello, my name is Albert Shansky).

He looked up with a startled expression, rose stiffly and stammered in perfect English.

"Good day to you Mr. Albert, I was waiting for you. I received a telephone call this morning from Mr. Takata to greet you when you arrive. I fear I missed your train and so waited for you in the hotel until you returned. My name is Hourani Kimiko. My friends call me Kim; *Yokoso*, welcome to Japan."

I extended my hand in western fashion, which he grabbed enthusiastically and began pumping.

"I am an agent for the Bristol-Myers Company and I would be most honored to be your host while you are in Hiroshima."

He delivered himself with precision, as if he had been called upon to make a public statement; and the balanced singsong neatness of his speech, occasionally corresponded to by a movement of his head was very conspicuous.

"Well that is a very generous offer and I am humbled by it."

"Shall we begin with an early dinner?"

"Yes, indeed. I am famished."

He looked at me with his doe-shaped eyes and began to speak with slow deliberate words," I know an excellent restaurant on the outskirts of the city called *Koryoriya*, a restaurant for traditional Japanese foods."

"Very good. Let us go."

We took a taxi at the front of the hotel and made our way through traffic to the restaurant within a half hour. The front of the restaurant at the door were several hanging purple curtains split in four parts and emblazoned in gold letters with the restaurant name in Kanji (Japanese characters). As we went inside a hostess wearing the typical traditional female kimono with a large rear obi greeted us, *"Okaeri nasai* (welcome)," she said with a deep bow.

After removing our shoes, we were led to a small private room with floor cushions on which we sat at a low table. The waitress brought each of us an *oshibori* (a rolled, damp washcloth for wiping hands and face). Then the waitress returned with a vase containing warm Sake (rice wine). She filled our small cups and retreated. Kim, my host, raised his cup and said in a low voice *kampai* (cheers). I followed suit and tasted the Sake, which startled me because of its unusual warm sweet taste.

"Is this your first experience with Sake?"

"Yes!"

Sake is a white wine made from fermented rice. Sake proudly claims an ancient history in Japan with strong religious and social meanings, which are still retained today. From the custom of offering sake as a libation to the gods, the drinking parties of today evolved. One of the distinctive features of Sake drinking is that Sake is warmed to about body temperature; this custom of warming Sake dates to about the Eighth Century.

A sense of community and sharing is expressed in a few "rules" about Sake drinking, which should be observed: one should never pour his own cup of Sake – rather another person fills your empty cup and you fill the cup of the other person? Similarly, the cup being filled should be held and not just left sitting on the table.

"Is Sake used on all social occasions?"

"The drinking of Sake has always been considered an essential part of every Japanese festival and ceremonial occasion and it is still offered to the gods and ancestors in community and household shrines. It is also the essential part of the nuptial pledge in traditional wedding ceremonies, in which the bride and groom drink three times from each of three ceremonial cups *(sansan kudo)."*

"Are there different grades of Sake?"

"There is a feeling that the best Sake comes from certain areas, usually in the colder North but unlike Western wines, Sake does not improve with age, and there are no "vintage years" for Sake."

Just then the waitress came in and carried on a quick conversation with Kim, my host.

"I have ordered for both of us. I hope I have not presumed too much."

"Not at all, it is better this way. I always have difficulty understanding the menu."

"I have ordered *Mizutaki* for the two of us."

The waitress brought in a large plate of chicken pieces, Chinese cabbage, leeks, tofu, and vermicelli, and placed it on the table. She then brought in an earthen pot containing a stock made from seaweed and dried fish shavings and set it to boil on a hot plate in the center of the table. Sitting on her knees in seiza position she cooked the chicken and vegetables a few at a time and placed them gingerly in our individual serving plates, as they were ready. A spicy sauce to be used as a dip was provided as well.

I began to eat the morsels accompanied by a bowl of steamed rice *(gohan)* and cups of green tea *(ryokucha).* For dessert we each had *anmitsu,* which is white gelatin cubes made from seaweed extract served with a scoop of sweet brown bean paste and a few pieces of Tientsin pears. A small container of honey was served with this dish to be used as a topping. I noticed Kim was eating the dessert with gusto. I could barely swallow it; it was so severely sweet. Albeit, the meal was an unusual culinary experience and I really enjoyed it.

I was getting a little tired of sitting on the cushion and so suggested to Kim that we depart for the hotel. He agreed and so I arose with difficulty since I had a sharp ache in the small of my back. I am always amazed when being entertained in Japan that I never see my host paying the bill. I suspect that some arrangement for payment is made beforehand in order to avoid embarrassment.

The hostess accompanied us outside with many bows where we found a taxi waiting. While riding back to the hotel I thanked Kim for a lovely dinner. He then started a conversation," What do you think of Hiroshima?"

"I am amazed at the quick recovery of the city." I hesitated for a moment and then added," I should like to apologize to you for the destruction to life and property by the atomic bomb."

"Thank you. Would you please accept my apology for the attack on Pearl Harbor?"

We continued small talk for a while and finally arrived at the hotel.

"May I pick you up tomorrow for breakfast?"

"That would be great. What time?"

"How about 8 o'clock?"

"See you then. Good night."

"Goodnight. Sleep well."

The next morning, I met Kim just outside the glass doorway to the hotel dining room.

"Have you been waiting long?"

"Not long, only a few minutes."

He responded with an indescribably charming smile. It was then that I noticed that Kim did not have the best of teeth; they were rather jagged and pale, lacking healthy luster and of that peculiar brittle translucence common among anemics.

"Shall we go in?"

"Of course, after you, please."

The house steward who gave each of us an American type menu seated us at a small table. The table was set in French style with crystal and silver service. The air was dominated by the solemn quiet great hotels pride themselves on. The waiters tiptoed back and forth serving the guests, and nothing could be heard beyond a rattle of a teapot and a half-whispered word. On our arrival the dining room was partially empty, although a few people did straggle in while we sat waiting for our order.

Sipping my tea, I watched as a tourist group turned up together with their guide. They were seated at a long table with much fanfare. Just then our breakfast arrived; mine consisting of French toast with syrup and bacon. Kim substituted pork sausages for the bacon and a jar of strawberry preserves substituted for the syrup. He spoke in a low almost inaudible voice, "Please permit me to show you the sights of the city today."

"Very well, I hope it is not too much trouble for you."

"Not at all, what I have in mind is a sort of walking tour. We will taxi to the Shukkeien Garden and then walk to the Hiroshima Castle and then take a taxi to Hijiyama Park and then to lunch at an *okonomiyaki* restaurant."

"Oh, it sounds wonderful. What is okonomiyaki?"

"You shall see. I think of it as a Japanese pizza pie."

II

The next morning Kim called on me at the hotel where we had breakfast. After breakfast Kim ordered a taxicab to take us to the Shukkeien Garden, which is not too far from Hiroshima Castle. Shukkeien Garden was constructed in 1620 as a villa for the Asano family, a feudal clan of Hiroshima. It is modeled on Xihu (West Lake) in China. A pond was in the center of the garden dotted with more than 10 islets of various sizes. Tea ceremony rooms and arbors are arranged among the islets. Footpaths connect these arbors. Kim and I strolled through these footpaths while enjoying the garden. I looked at him with a rapt smile on my face. "Isn't it beautiful, Kim?"

He returned the smile. "Yes, indeed. I can imagine the serenity experienced by Lord Asano as he walked among these islets."

We left Shukkeien Garden and walked to the Hiroshima Castle. The Hiroshima Castle, as it stands today, is a reproduction of the donjon, which belonged to the original castle; the original went down to ashes by the atomic bomb. The three floors of the castle contained art objects, Asano family artifacts, photos, writings, maps and armory. It became rather fatiguing viewing it all but at the same time it was extremely interesting to see the state of feudalism in medieval Japan.

We left the castle to take a taxi to Hijiyama Park. By this time I was very torpid and suggested that we rest in a teahouse located on the hill in the park. The taxi drove us to a summit of the small hill where one can obtain a fine view of most of the city. The hillside is covered with multitudes of cherry trees. Unfortunately cherry blossoms were not blooming at this time.

After resting and sipping tea we strolled around the park. There were many other people strolling as well, some taking photos others viewing the plantings and flowers. Several groups of elderly women were strolling with parasols. At this time, I became very tired and suggested having lunch. Kim agreed and found a taxicab to take us to the restaurant to eat "okonomiyaki".

Kim looked at me with amazement as he spoke, "Are you ready for Japanese pizza?"

"Of course, what is okonomiyaki?"

"It consists of cabbage, some vegetables, seafood, meat, an egg and soba or udon noodles all piled on a thin plate sized crepe and then fried on a grill."

I listened in wonderment. "Wow, it sounds wonderful. Let's order."

Kim ordered and suggested Sapporo beer as a beverage. I nodded in agreement. It was a very filling meal, which I could barely finish. I looked at Kim with a satisfying Cheshire cat grin. *"Oishi!, it* was delicious."

Kim smiled at me as we sipped our beer. I then looked at him while I spoke," Thank you for your kindness to me. But now I would like to return to the hotel and make plans for my departure tomorrow."

We shook hands in American style and took leave of each other. I went back to my room and napped for two hours dreaming about my forthcoming adventure on the Inland Sea. I must have been very tired because I fell asleep almost immediately.

Suddenly, there was a sharp knock on the door, which woke me out of my oneiric state.

"Who is it?" I asked with a shout. Someone answered in Japanese. *"Sumimasen Shanskysan."*

I went to the door and discovered a young Japanese boy dressed in a uniform standing at the threshold holding a package wrapped in a *furoshiki.* He handed it to me with a low bow. I took it into the room wondering what it contained. I unfolded the furoshiki and found a note lying on top of the box, which read:

Goodbye Shanskysan. May your journey be enjoyable and fruit-ful? Kim

I was taken aback by this kind sentiment and proceeded to open the box. Lo and behold! It contained a pocketknife (a Japanese version of the Swiss Army pocketknife), a compass, a magnifying glass and a small leather bound Japanese-English dictionary. All the items one needs for travel of an uncertain nature and destiny.

I was touched by his delicate sensibility. But then again it is traditional for Japanese to give presents when visiting and for those departing on journeys. Even the furoshiki, which was made of fine habutae silk, will make a nice present for my wife who can use it for a head- scarf.

I sat down on the floor and began to plan out my next moves in criss-crossing the Inland Sea. After consulting a map, I noticed to my great disappointment that I would not be able to visit Matsue, which is another one hour run by train from Izumo, a town down the coast a little way beyond the port of Hagi.

Matsue is associated with the American writer Lafcaido Hearn who lived there at the end of the last century. His old home is still preserved. His name is greatly revered by Japanese students of English. There is no doubt that he loved and understood Japan. I have one of his books, *Kwaidan,* in my home library. It is a gothic compilation of strange and weird things.

I decided to go out for dinner before retiring. I found a small restaurant not too far from the hotel. It seemed inviting so I went in and ordered Yakitori and gohan (fried chicken and boiled rice). I enjoyed it even though I wasn't too hungry after the big lunch of Japanese pizza pie.

III

The most beautiful of all the islands of the Inland Sea is Miyajima with soaring, mountainous landscape and luxurious vegetation. I rode a bus from Hiroshima to Miyajima-guchi on the shore opposite the island, in about an hour. By this route I was able to enjoy some superb views of the islands and the oyster and seaweed beds with their floating rafts and serried ranks of bamboo stakes, as well as some attractive little fishing harbors. A small ferryboat took me across to the island of Miyajima.

Miyajima is most famous for its ancient shrine, founded by the Heike clan in the days of their greatness before their defeat and eventual downfall after the battle with the Genji clan at Dan-no-ura. The huge *torii*, known as Itsukushima, stands off shore and appeared to me to float on the water. I remember, fondly, the sudden appearance of a deer strolling into the restaurant where I was eating lunch. They are unafraid of humans and come into the restaurant for handouts from patrons. I offered a handful of cooked rice to one that approached me. It was quickly devoured from my open palm.

After lunch I registered and got settled in the hotel. I then went outside to explore a little. A cable car took me to the summit of Mount Misen. The views of the Inland Sea from there were incredibly beautiful; especially viewing the red maple leaves in Maple Valley. Next, I visited a small temple of the Shingon sect near the top of Mount Misen where I was fortunate to witness a fire walking ceremony.

A bonfire of cypress branches is lit and afterwards the priest and those of the faithful who wish to ensure good health for the coming year walked over the still smoldering ashes in bare feet. I winced with every step they took.

The primeval forest on the summit of Mt. Misen is preserved as a natural monument. I was able to see a splendid view of Hiroshima City, the nearby mountains and the Inland Sea with its innumerable islets. After a while I took the ropeway down to Momijidani station and walked to Miyajima pier. I then followed a road for about 10 minutes to the Five-storied Pagoda, the Itsukushima Shrine, Daigan-ji temple and Tahoto Pagoda.

The Itsukushima Shrine presently consists of the Main Shrine and several subsidiary shrines and buildings – all connected by wide corridors or galleries. These stretch above the sea on both sides of the shrine. I stood there watching as the tide came in. The whole edifice seemed to begin floating. These shrines have been designated as National Treasures. As I walked along the corridor in front of the shrine I was able to view an exhibit of the utensils and sacred vessels used in Shinto worship.

I, next, went to Iwakuni, on the mainland of Honshu by bus. It was a most memorable trip because I had an opportunity to speak with a friendly gentleman in the next seat in English and my broken Japanese.

Iwakuni is a small town immensely proud of its Kintai-bashi, or Bridge of the Brocaded Sash. This bridge was originally built in 1673 by a local baron, Kikkawa Hiroyoshi. One story relates that once when he was baking rice-cakes the cakes curled upward and gave him the idea for the shape of the bridge. The bridge, 750 feet long, is made of wood, in five high, gracefully arched spans on stone piers. In the evening I was able to watch cormorant fishing from the bridge. This fishing method is said to be about 200 years old and is still in use today.

Ogori, 57 miles from Iwakuni, is the station for Yamaguchi, which I reached in 10 minutes by taxi. On the way I passed through Yuda, a spa of more than local reputation and large enough to keep more than a hundred geisha employed. I remained here and was able to take advantage of their renowned body scrub and massage. My room was in a typical Japanese Ryokan where I slept on a futon on the floor.

Yamaguchi itself is a small city cherishing a few relics of a glorious past. The Sesshu Garden, which was originally planned by a great 15th century landscape artist, has been altered but it is still beautiful. After a short stop I proceeded onward to Shimonoseki, which lies at the tip of Honshu. I reached it the next morning by a fast train. It is here that I tasted Fugu (blow fish), which is poisonous in its unprepared state. I must admit that I didn't care for it, or maybe I was apprehensive and somewhat frightened by its toxic reputation.

The port of Hagi is a fascinating and well-preserved example of a samurai town of the Edo period. Hagi ware, which originated as an imitation of 16th century Korean pottery, is greatly prized by lovers of the tea ceremony. While there I purchased a cup made of brown earthenware, which I now use for pencils on my desk at home.

In the evening I boarded a large boat with many passengers of every description, which took me as well the other passengers to the city of Matsuyama on the island of Shikoku, one of the four main islands of Japan. This is the first crossing of the Inland Sea I was to make.

All during the crossing I stood on deck looking at the lights on the boats plying across the sea. I imagined they were flashing fireflies because I could not make out the outline of the boats in the dark night. Close to morning I went below deck to sleep on the floor with a provided blanket. The snoring and breathing noises of the other passengers did not disturb my sleep of a couple of hours before landing at Matsuyama.

It was nearly sunrise when I arrived; bleary eyed, at Okudogo, one of the better Japanese style establishments at Dogo Hot Springs in Matsuyama's suburbs. Like most of the other modern inns, it looked like a Western hotel from the outside. Several stories of concrete and glass faced me as I entered, Inside, however, I found purely Japanese style rooms, fair gardens, and several baths, public and private, in which I could enjoy the hot sulphur waters of Dogo

Onsen. I look forward to this because there is little to do in the hot springs suburb itself.

Matsuyama is the capital city of Ehime Prefecture, which boasts some of the most colorful folk art, has a well-preserved castle and cherry-filled parks in addition to the alkaline springs at Dogo. Also, I expect to visit Omogo Valley, 32 miles away, which is famous for the weird beauty of its maple trees.

The first thing I did the next day was to attend one of the public hot sulphur baths. As I approached the building, I noticed two separate entrances with signs. One marked MEN and the other marked WOMEN in Japanese. Obviously, I went through the one-marked MEN but was startled to find, once inside, that women were coming in from the other entrance and began to mingle with the men. I was somewhat dismayed but carried on nevertheless.

There were hooks on the wall to place removed clothing and men and women intermixed in the large tiled hot tub in the nude. Men kept some distance from the women, and every one was chatting away as if nothing unusual was occurring. After a half hour in the tub, I was not the least bit embarrassed but I could not stand the awful smell of the water. I left to take a shower and leave.

I went back to the hotel to have lunch. I was seated by the waitress at a single table and given a menu to peruse. Since it was written in Japanese I found it confusing and difficult to discern. There were, however, some pictures of local culinary delights. I was just about to order when an elderly gentleman approached my table. He held his hand on the other chair as he addressed me in perfect English, "May I join you?"

I rose slightly and gestured to the chair, "Of course, please do."

"You are American?"

"Hai. Watakushi no namei Shansky Albert."

"Ha! Ha! You speak Japanese very well."

"No. No. I was just being polite. I do not speak Japanese at all. But, I am learning."

"Well, my name is Takahira Kenji. You may call me Ken."

I responded with an outstretched hand, "You may call me Al."

We shook hands while both beaming. He continued talking as if an explanation was needed.

"I noticed you in the public bath and thought: *that man is American.* You seemed so lonely and out of place that I felt I should approach you and put you at your ease."

"Thank you. It was quite an unusual experience. Tell me. Where did you learn English?"

"I learned in school but I really honed and whetted my skill at work."

"Did you say work?"

"Yes, I work at the U. S. Embassy in Tokyo as a translator and interpreter."

"I see. You speak as well as a Native American. Have you ever been to America?"

"No. But someday I hope to go to Boston. My son is studying engineering at MIT."

"Really? How wonderful. Give me his address and telephone number and I shall call him when I return. I live in Connecticut, but I have two children in school in Boston."

"Oh, thank you. That would be very nice. I hope it is not too much trouble for you."

He took out a pen and pad from his jacket breast pocket and began writing on a sheet. Finally, he tore the sheet out of the pad and handed it to me.

"This is very nice of you. I hope it is not too much trouble for you."

"Not at all, it is my pleasure."

There was silence for a moment then he began speaking again, "May I help you with the menu?"

"Oh please. What is this picture on the menu?"

I was pointing to a picture of what appeared to be different colored balls, skewered three on a stick.

"Let me see. Oh yes. Those are Botchan dumplings. They are moist and sweet."

"Sounds good! I think I'll have that with a pot of ryokucha (green tea)."

"Is that all?"

"Yes. I want to save my appetite for dinner."

He looked at me oddly with a whimsical combination of familiar facial expressions, "Those snacks were named "Botchan-Dango" because Soseki Natsume, author of the novel "Botchan" used to enjoy them when he worked at Matsuyama Junior High School." "I read several books by Soseki Natsume and enjoyed them immensely. I particularly liked, Kokoro, a tragic story of an intellectual forced by his own devotion to everyday obligations to a pointless and thwarted life."

"Do you read many Japanese authors?"

"Yes. I've read Kawabata, Kobo Abe, And Kafu the scribbler as well as Soseki Natsume. I enjoyed them all. "

I could see the waitress approaching our table. She bowed slightly and spoke in Japanese almost *sotto voce, "Tetsudau kudasai.* (May I help you please?)"

Ken began ordering in Japanese as the waitress simultaneously was saying Hai, Hai, and Hai. The waitress then left with a slight bow. Then Ken spoke to me in a quizzical manner. "Do you have any plans for this afternoon?"

I answered, "None in particular, just some sightseeing."

"Well, I am going to the Ishite Temple. Would you like to join me? We can share taxicab to take us there."

"Sounds good! What is the Ishite Temple?"

"It's the 51st of the Shikoku temples."

"Forgive me. I do not understand."

"There are 88 temples dispersed on the periphery of Shikoku. The monk Kukai, whose honorific name is Kobo Daishi, in order to propagate Shingon Buddhism, built these temples in the 8th century. Devoted people go on a pilgrimage by walking around the island and visiting all 88 temples."

"All 88 temples? How long does it take?"

"It takes about a month or more."

"Are you on the pilgrimage?"

He responded with light laughter, "Ha! Ha! No, No. I am a simple tourist like you on vacation. But come along with me. Within the temple structures are many National treasures and important cultural properties."

"I would be delighted to accompany you. It sounds most intriguing."

After lunch, Ken ordered a cab to take us to Ishite Temple. While in the cab he spoke about the Dogo Hot Springs. "Did you enjoy the hot sulphur bath?"

"Not really. The smell annoyed me."

"Were you embarrassed about the presence of naked women in the tub? Most Westerners are shy about this."

"At first I felt modest but I got used to it eventually and then thought nothing of it, except when I got out of the tub and exposed myself."

"Spas are beginning to separate men and women these days. I believe this is the last of the communal baths. You know, of course, that there are some public toilets that are communal."

"Yes, I've used them."

Ken began to change the subject. "Anyhow, the Dogo Hot Springs is the oldest in Japan. It's about 3000 years old. Legend has it that in the age of the Gods, a white heron healed its injured leg in the waters gushing out of a crevice in the rocks. That is why it is called "Kami-no-yu", water of the Gods."

We then arrived at the Ishite Temple and found many people milling about. I saw some wearing a distinctive white uniform with special hat and leggings and carrying a staff. Ken leaned over to me to explain their presence in a whisper. "They are pilgrims making the trip around Shikoku."

I saw some of these people approaching a monk carrying a sheet of paper to which the monk applied a seal. I nudged Ken with a question, "What is that about?"

"The paper is called a Fuda on which is printed a map of Shikoku containing the 88 temples to which the monk of each temple applies his seal."

"I see, that then becomes evidence of having made the trip."

"More or less, when we finish here would you like to visit the Matsuyama Castle?"

"Yes, indeed. That would be fine. "

So once again we took a taxicab on our way to the castle.

While in the taxicab, I questioned Ken, "Are you religious, Ken?"

He looked at me with a hesitant stare, "Well, I believe so."

"What is your religion?"

"I am a Buddhist."

"Really! I am very interested in Buddhism. Please tell me about it."

"I don't know what to say. There are many sects of Buddhism. I belong to the Soto Zen sect. My temple is Soji-ji in Yokohama. It is the third most important Zen temple in Japan."

"Are there others?"

"Yes. The leading temple is Eiheiji and the second is Hosshinji, both in Fukui Prefecture just north of Kyoto."

"Is your whole family Buddhist?"

He hung his head before responding, "My wife toyed with Christianity for a while before she died but eventually remained a Buddhist. She also attended a Shinto temple after our marriage. Her ashes were buried with a Buddhist ceremony in a Buddhist graveyard."

"I am sorry about your wife's death. What was her ailment, if I may ask?"

"She died of cancer."

"Your son is your only child?"

"Yes."

He looked at me questioningly, "Are you Christian?"

"No. I am Jewish."

"Yes, I know. One of the American workers at the Embassy is Jewish."

Quickly changing the subject I brought forth more questions," What is the main tenet of Buddhism?"

He became pensive for a while then began slowly to reiterate, "I suppose one could say that it is the Buddhist Doctrine of Impermanence."

"Did you say impermanence? How is that?"

Once again he became reticent before answering, "As is well known, the doctrine of *anicca* (impermanence), along with those of *dukkha* (suffering) and *anatta* (no-self) constitutes one of the three marks of existence (*tilakhana*) according to Buddhism."

"But what makes impermanence so important."

"The manner in which such impermanence has been understood by and large in Buddhism may be described as ontological. In other words, the doctrine emphasizes the fact that the universe, and the objects it contains, is impermanent. The ontological thrust of the regnant understanding is clear from the fact that it led to the formulation of the doctrine of momentariness or *ksanikavada* or the doctrine that the final reality about the universe boils down to a concatenation of discrete flashes of reality."

"I find it difficult to follow. I am still not sure I understand the importance of impermanence as a doctrine."

"It might be worth supplementing this understanding with a psychological one. For if everything is impermanent then it applies as much to mental as physical states. This approach links it with the concept of *anatta* or the view that there is no permanent substratum of any kind underlying the subjective individual, just as there is not permanent stratum of any kind underlying the objective universe."

"I think I'm lost. It's much too deep for me. Isn't the individual important in Buddhism?"

"Yes, indeed. In this formulation, however, the doctrine still remains ontological in its orientation. There is an exception, however.

It is now applied towards understanding the nature of the subjective individual, just as I have addressed the question of the constitution of the objective universe."

Just then the taxicab came to a stop and we alighted before the Matsuyama Castle. I turned to Ken with a low sounding assertion." I see I have much to learn. "

He looked at me for a moment and began offering advice with some authority in his voice. "If you really want to learn about Buddhism you should go to a training monastery such as Hosshinji in Obama. I spent three months there."

"Was that before or after your wife died?"

"It was just after. I felt I needed some solacement and consolation at the time. It certainly helped me overcome my bereavement."

We started walking slowly down the gravel path as we talked. The grinding gravel beneath our feet emphasized the severity of our conversation.

"You said your wife was interested in Christianity. Could you tell me about it?"

"I think she was greatly influenced by some of her friends who felt the need to pray to a God. She tried it on occasion by going to church with them but apparently it did not satisfy her."

"It did not? I am curious, why not?"

"Well she was brought up as a Buddhist and we were married in a Shinto temple. In Buddhism there is no God and for that matter there is no Soul and no Hereafter. Buddhism is a non-substantial religion whereas Christianity is substantial since it believes that a God exists. This confliction troubled her."

"I see. So, she did not continue?"

"That's right. She did not continue."

By this time we came to the front entrance of Matsuyama Castle, at which point there seemed to be a congruency of our thoughts.

IV

On returning to the Dogo Spa we made some plans while riding in a taxicab. I proffered him in a very friendly manner with a proposal, "Ken, I am leaving tomorrow, what are your plans?"

Without hesitation he said, "I am leaving as well. I intend taking the train to Imabari; then a boat to Omishima Island for a look at the Oyamazumi Shrine and then a hydrofoil to Ikuchijima Island to inspect the Kosanji Temple; then a boat to Mihara where I can pick up the bullet train (Shinkansen) to Tokyo."

"It sounds very exciting. May I join you?"

"Of course."

"Well, at least, I can accompany you until Kurashki on the bullet train."

He responded with a broad grin, "That would be very nice."

Soon we arrived at the hotel of the Dogo Hot Springs. We departed for our respective rooms after arranging to meet for dinner in the evening. It's been a very long day and when I reached my room I suddenly became very tired. I attempted to take a nap. But, sleep eluded me so I resorted to day dreaming and reviewing the events of the day and anticipating the coming days of adventure as I lay on my futon. I washed and dressed for the evening meal. Later, I met Ken in the dining room.

"Konbonwa. Good evening."

"Yes. Yes. Good evening."

We entered the room and sat on cushions before a low table. The waitress submissively approached and spoke *sotto voce* with Ken. Ken looked at me seemingly seeking my approval.

"Would you like *Gempei Nabe?* It appears to be a specialty of the house."

"Yes, of course. It sounds most inviting. But, what is it."

"It is a pot dish that originated from the dish that the Genji clan ate to celebrate their victory over the Heike clan. It is full of fresh seafood and vegetables."

"Sounds great!"

The waitress filled our cups with sake and we toasted each other. *Kampai.* The warm liquid moved smoothly down my throat with uninterrupted motion. I really enjoyed the effect.

I asked Ken, "How far is Imabari from here?"

He thought for a moment then replied with some hesitation, "Oh about 120 kilometers or about 70 miles, distances are usually measured in the metric system; sometimes old Japanese measurements called *shaku* are used, and distances are not always accurate when converted into miles."

After a very satisfying meal we each entered our separate rooms after making up to meet the next morning to take a taxi to the JR train station. Ken explained that we could order breakfast on the train, which seemed very convenient. Thus the night ended.

Standing on the train platform with our luggage at 9:13 the next morning for the quick ride to Imabari seemed like one more segment in my adventure on the Inland Sea. The train was on time. We boarded and occupied two seats with a fold-down table between us. Suddenly, a cart came rolling through the aisle selling tea, fried dumplings, and rice porridge (*congee*). In 45 minutes we arrived in Imabari, rested and sated.

Imabari is a rather squalid seaport town of about 100,000 people on the Inland Sea in Ehime Prefecture. Its one great treasure is Imabari Castle, which is a rare example of a coastal *hirajiro* type castle (one built in an open plain). The castle tower serves as an exhibition room and observation platform, which provides a splendid view of the islands of the Inland Sea. Ken and I began to look for the ferry, which would take us to the island of Omishima. We eventually arrived at dockside, which appeared defective and broken down through neglect.

The day was sunny and warm when we boarded the ferry- boat. Having settled ourselves on deck at the bow we waited for the boat to sail and the voyage to begin. People were coming aboard – mostly working people and some tourists. Almost all lined the periphery of the top deck occupying the wooden benches along the safety railing. In addition, the aft of the boat was loaded with many boxes of goods for transport to the island. With a loud roar of its engines the boat got underway. The vessel managed to get out to the deep water and then navigate in a northward direction.

The day was beautiful with scudding clouds against the cerulean blue hue of the clear sky. The blue sea gave the impression that we were floating between two worlds. Suddenly a young chap began playing a shakahachu (bamboo flute). The music wafted by like perfume and some people began singing softly. The lyrics were Japanese and the songs were unknown to me. But the songs seemed familiar to Ken who began mouthing the words intermittently. In a short while we approached the verdant shore of Omishima Island. The boat began to dock and people were rising and fidgeting in preparation for the landing. The gangway was let down with a loud thud and people began scurrying off. Ken and I were among the last to debark. While carrying our luggage we sought out a taxicab to take us to the Oyamazumi Shrine. All we could find was a bicycle rickshaw. So this would have to do.

The Oyamazumi Shrine has many fascinating structures such as the *honden* (main sanctuary), which was rebuilt during the Muromachi Period (1392-1573), and the *homotsukan* (treasure museum), which displays many national treasures. Oyamazumi Shrine is a shrine to the gods of the sea and mountain and has been a place of worship since ancient times. It is said that approximately 80% of the nation's historical arms, armor and helmets, which are designated as national treasures are kept in this museum.

After the conclusion of our visit to the Oyamazumi Shrine we set about walking across Omishima Island to the dock of the hydrofoil, which would take us to Ikuchijima Island where we intended visiting Kosanji Temple and Museum. Kosanji Temple has numerous examples of Japanese architecture.

The walk was arduous because we had to carry our luggage. For me it was not that difficult because my one bag had a shoulder strap enabling me to carry it without too much difficulty. But Ken had two duffel bags with handles, which caused great carrying difficulty for him. As a result we were required to stop and rest many times on our walk.

Finally, we reached the hydrofoil dock and were told that the hydrofoil would not leave for an hour. We then decided to get some lunch at a small roadside stand. We each ordered a small plate of Izushi soba noodles. Soba noodles are made from powdered buckwheat. Izushi soba is a type of noodle unique to Japan, and is eaten by dipping in sweet soy sauce mixed with a raw quail egg.

After lunch we walked along the shore having left our bags with the dock attendant. We reached a sand dune dotted with grass clumps and sat down to view the beautiful sea. We watched a band of small shorebirds conversing together as they run about on the level sand. It reminded me of the lovely Haiku poem by Buson (eighteenth century).

Shigi toku

Kuwa susugu

Mizo-no uneri kana

Afar, shorebirds are flying

Near, the water ripples,

Washing the hoe.

I broke the silence by asking Ken about Buddhism.

"Ken, are there any other major tenets of Buddhism besides impermanence?"

He seemed to be jolted out of his oneiric state, "There are many. Let me see. Yes, of course. There is emptiness."

"Did you say emptiness?"

26

"Yes, emptiness or Voidness, it is known as *shunyata.*"

I shook my head in disbelief and said in a somewhat startled voice, "Please explain."

He began speaking slowly but soon rattled on, "Emptiness or Voidness is that which stands right in the middle between affirmation and negation, existence and non-existence."

"I don't understand. Please continue."

"The void is all-inclusive; having no opposite, there is nothing, which it excludes or opposes. It is living void, because all forms come out of it, and whoever realizes the void is filled with life and power and the love of all beings."

I was astounded and could only retort, "Do you really believe that?"

He quickly responded in a severe voice, "Indeed, I do."

I waited for a moment unable to gather my immediate thoughts.

"But that doesn't sound like religion."

He hesitated a moment but looked me straight in the eye with his response, "Religiosity results from a group of innate psychological faculties, each of which has evolved to help deal with existential human dilemmas like death, pain, and loneliness."

I looked at his eyes, which were surrounded by epicanthic folds. I thought, there are few better lenses to the soul than the eyes. There appeared lacunae in our conversation but I continued," I don't mean to be stubbornly resistant. I can understand impermanence. We grow old. Things decay. Nothing stays the same. But emptiness is a horse of a different color.

"Ha. Ha. Well put. The term *shunyata* or emptiness is used primarily in connection with the 'no-self' *(anatman)* doctrine to denote that the Five Aggregates *(skandhas)* are 'empty' of the permanent self or soul which is erroneously imputed to them"

With a shake of my head I muttered, "I see. I see."

He continued in a pedantic manner, "By extension the term came to be applied to reality as a whole just as the individual is 'void' of a self, in the sense of an unchanging controlling agency, so too is the whole universe 'void' of a self or anything belonging to a self."

"Whoa. What are the Five Aggregates?"

He answered straightforwardly without pause.

"In Buddhism the five aggregations compose or constitute human appearance. They are: material composition *(rupa)*, sensing *(vedana)*, perception *(samjna)*, mental formations *(samskara)*, and consciousness *(vijnana)*."

I was taken aback and non-plussed as I watched him recite while counting on five fingers.

"Wow! I find that very difficult to understand. I am afraid you lost me."

He looked at me while reflecting, "It took me many years to understand the concept. Don't be in a hurry. You must think about it long and hard. Remember life is about refinement not perfection."

I hung my head and thought to myself – *I must get a book or have someone explain it to me.*

Ken looked at me with a deliberate strain in his eyes and a voice inflection, which expressed the obvious, "There is a book written by Dogen Zenji in the 13ᵗʰ century. It is called the Shobogenzo and has become for Zen Buddhists the equivalent of the Bible for Christians. There is a part of the Shobogenzo called the Genjokoan. I think its teachings can be of help to you. I remember some of it and probably can paraphrase much of it. Would you like me to recite parts to you?"

I responded with a common exclamation of surprise, "Oh, yes. I would be very grateful."

He cleared his throat and started to speak slowly, "The Genjokoan was originally a letter, which Dogen wrote to a lay disciple. It has become the first chapter of the Shobogenzo. Its teachings examine our everyday life, pointing out that the very barriers hindering us are the gates leading us to freedom."

With an anxious voice I said, "I see."

Ken took a deep breath and continued, "When all things are Buddha Dharma, there is delusion and enlightenment, practice, life, death, all Buddhas, and sentient beings. When all dharmas are without self, there is no delusion, no enlightenment, no Buddhas, no sentient beings, no birth and no decay. Because the Buddha Way is beyond abundance and lack, there is birth and decay, delusion and enlightenment, beings and Buddhas. Nevertheless, flowers fall while we admire them and weeds flourish to our chagrin. OK, so far."

"Yes. Yes. But what does it mean?"

Ken started again with some emotional feeling." To carry you forward and experience myriad things is delusion. For myriad things to come forth and experience themselves is realization."

He stopped for a moment then looking in my eyes he continued." In seeing forms by mustering body-mind and hearing sounds by mustering body-mind, although you grasp things directly, it is not like an image reflected in the mirror or the moon in the water. When one side is illuminated, the other is dark."

I raised my hand and asked him, "Is body-mind a single entity?"

"Yes," he said with emphasis.

"OK then. Please continue."

He simply picked up where he left off as if there was no interruption." To study the Buddha Way is to study oneself. To study oneself is to forget the self. To forget the self is to be confirmed by myriad things. Being confirmed by myriad things is to cast off body-mind of self as well as body-mind of others. No trace of realization remains, and this traceless state continues endlessly."

I raised my hand again and asked, "Is realization enlightenment?"

Ken responded with a unique cognitive comprehension. "Yes. Someone attaining awakening is like the moon reflected on the water. The moon does not get wet, nor is the water broken. Although its light is broad and diffuse, the moon is reflected even in a puddle an inch wide. The whole moon and the entire sky are reflected in dew-drops on the grass, or even in one drop of water. Awakening does not divide the person, just as the moon does not break the water. The awakening of a person cannot be obstructed, just as a drop of water does not obstruct the moon in the sky. The depth of the drop is the height of the moon. Each reflection, however, long or short its duration, or however large or small the body of water, realizes the limitlessness of the moonlight in the sky."

I was startled by the allegorical use of the moon in his discussion. I approached him again, "Boy, that's a useful metaphor to talk about enlightenment. What is the limit of perception?"

He took a deep breath, rubbed his nose, and continued. "When you have still not fully realized the Dharma in body-mind you think it sufficient. When the dharma fills body-mind, you feel some lack. For example, when you take a boat to sea, where mountains are out of sight, and look around, you see only roundness; you cannot see anything else. But this great ocean is neither round nor square. Its other characteristics are countless. Some see it as a palace, others as an ornament. We only see it as round for the time being – within the field of our vision: this is the way we see all things."

For a while neither of us said anything. I just kept shaking my head affirmatively up and down saying, "Thank you. Thank you."

V

We rose off our spots on the sand dune and proceeded to the hydrofoil. Once again a large contingent of people boarded the streamlined boat. Everyone climbed to the top deck, which was protected from the spume and water spray by a series of plastic windows surrounding the periphery. A loud noise indicated that the boat was about to depart.

It lifted out of the water and shot out into the sea with a lurch and great force. The spumescence of the water hitting the plastic windows prevented good views of the surrounding sea but the speed was thrilling nevertheless.

We arrived on Ikuchijima Island in less than twenty minutes. Once again after debarking we arranged for a taxicab to take us to Kosanji Temple. Ken explained the name of the temple to me as we walked up the pathway to the front entrance. Ko means old, san means mountain, and ji means temple; so in Japanese Kosanji means Old Mountain Temple.

Kosanji Temple was constructed over a period exceeding thirty years. The temple precincts cover over 45,000 acres and feature various gates, halls, and pagodas. We did not have time to see it all so we concentrated on the main building. The appearance of the main building had a decided Chinese influence. It was a center for institutionalized Buddhist practice. Apparently this temple and other Japanese Buddhist temples, both architecturally and religiously, were heavily influenced in the 6th to 8th century by the Chinese and Korean temple systems.

At the heart of most temples in Japan is the enshrined figure of some particular Buddha, Bodhisattva, Saint or historical founder, which gives the temple its unique religious character. We were able to see the large Buddha enshrined within and at the attached museum viewed the artifacts associated with the temple.

The taxicab, which was waiting for us, took us to the next boat dock for the final leg of our journey across the Inland Sea.

We boarded the boat at 2:30 in the afternoon with a crowd of commuters who rushed to the top deck for the 25- minute ride to Mihara. As the boat sailed across the smooth, azure-like waters we saw many little islands, which randomly dotted the sea. These are considered the first bit of Japan to be created from the union of Izanagi and Izanami, the legendary god and goddess who created all the Japanese people and their islands, the latter forming in the water from divine seminal droppings.

The misty peaks of Honshu were visible in the distance as we came into shore. We only had about 45 minutes to wait for the bullet train, so we had no time to explore Mihara other than to grab a quick bite at the train station. The train was scheduled to leave at 3:43 and arrive in Kurashiki at 4:13 in the afternoon, where Ken and I would part with a farewell after our Levantine trip.

As usual the train arrived on time and we boarded with our luggage. Finding two seats together, we sat quiescently in order to allow the weariness to dissipate. My inactivity suddenly made me aware of an urgent need to urinate. I got up, excusing myself from Ken, and went in search of the WC. I found it and locked myself in. There in front of me above the commode was a series of instructional pictures. I could not decipher the Japanese characters but the pictures were obviously explanatory. Japanese men and women traditionally sit on their haunches over a china vessel to urinate. The pictures were showing the proper western way; that one should not sit on their haunches on the seat of the commode. I thought this to be very comical and hurried back to tell Ken.

Ken laughed with me and said, "It takes sometime to get rid of old habits."

The train, following the old Tokaido road, was rushing along through a sylvan part of the shoreline. Since we were hading east

I was able to view the Inland Sea from our window. One could see many small boats plying there way across the rippling water which tossed them up and down like bobbing corks, leaving a broken wake of foam in their trail.

After a deliberate forbearance of speech, I broke the silence by speaking to Ken, "I want to thank you, Ken, for allowing me to accompany you on this trip."

He shrugged his shoulders and raised both his hands in the gesture of nothingness, "It was my pleasure."

I continued as he dismissed my words. "I hope I was not too much of a burden to you in asking questions about Buddhism. What you told me made a deep impression on me."

"Think nothing of it. I enjoyed speaking about Buddhism. I hope I was able to help you."

He appeared weary so I felt it was time to change the subject. "Are you looking forward to seeing your wife?"

He looked up as if alerted by the question. "Yes, indeed."

To continue the conversation, I said, "There's an old saying – 'it's nice to go away but it is nicer to come back'."

"Oh, how true."

"I'll be leaving you at Kurashiki. May we exchange cards? It is my fond wish to keep in contact with you. Would that please you?"

"Of course, of course it would."

We exchanged cards and shook hands. Ken then asked me, "Where do you go after Kurashiki?"

I answered, "From Kurashiki I go 10 miles to Okayama; then back by boat through Uno to Takamatsu in Shikoku. I will then take a boat to Osaka and from Osaka fly to Tokyo where I intend visiting Chichibu and then to Narita for the trip home."

After a tearful goodbye, I got off the train in Kurashiki. I felt a momentary loneliness and stood still until I could establish what to do next. I had an omen of good things to come as I looked for a taxi-cab to take me to the Hotel Kurashiki Kokusai. Once I got settled I decided to go for a walk around town. The hotel being centrally located, more or less, gave me the opportunity to look at the shops. As I passed a bakery (*panya*) a woman wearing a white apron and with a white head- scarf came running out to greet me.

"Yokoso! Yokoso!" (Welcome)

I stopped in my tracks and turned to receive her. She extended her arm to show me; in her hand she carried what looked like a beignet or a long, narrow French bread wrapped in a tissue paper. She spoke to me in relatively good English. "Please have this bread, dear sir. Today is our first day in making Western baked goods."

I hesitated as she offered the bread, *"Arigato"* (Thank you), I said as I took the proffered bread.

By way of explanation, she said, "It is a custom to give gifts of ones produce on the first day."

I understood this was a tradition and repeated my limited words, "Thank you."

She immediately responded, "My husband learned Western baking in Bombay, India and that is where I learned to speak English."

I wished the couple much luck and kept on walking. Eventually, I came upon a large looking building of Greek architecture. I kept staring at it until, after questioning a pedestrian, I learned it was the Ohara Gallery of Art Museum. I sat down on a bench in front of the museum and began to sketch the edifice while nibbling on the French bread. I had brought along a sketchpad and a No. 2 drawing pencil, which I always carry when I travel.

A few young kids and some adults surrounded me as I worked at my drawing. A low buzz of voices arose as I continued with my task. I found the presence of these people disturbing so I completed my drawing and approached the entrance to the museum. The museum was closed that day. I vowed to return the next day.

I was not hungry for dinner having devoured most of the bread. It was early so I decided to follow the canal, which flowed in front of the Ohara Museum. During the Edo Period (1603-1868), the historical area along the canal was directly governed by the Tokugawa Shogunate as a distribution center primarily for rice, it now housed in remodeled former rice granaries, the Museum of Folk craft, the Archeological Museum and many others revealing Kurashiki's past. The canal reminded me of Amsterdam, particularly since there were willow trees planted along the side edges along with some stone lanterns and memorial stele. Kurashiki is renowned for the excellent Folk craft Museums, which stand opposite one another on either side of the town's willow-lined canal. This is the canal up which boats used to come from the Inland Sea to be loaded with grain for Osaka. From four of these old rice granaries the present Folk craft Museum was built in 1948. The interior is worth observing for its own sake, especially the huge pine beams which run the length of the upper rooms. The exhibits include utensils of daily use from Japan and abroad. Their beauty, simplicity, and above all their practicality emphasize the best elements common to handicraft throughout the world.

The next day, I returned to the Ohara Museum of Art. The museum was established in 1930, and was the first gallery of Western art in Japan. The main building, designed after a Greek temple, can be found more than 140 paintings by great European masters such as El Greco, Monet, Matisse, Renoir, Gaugin and Picasso. A little way down the canal I stopped in to see the Shinkeien Garden and then the Ninagawa Museum.

The gardens of Japan are spectacular. They are designed to have flowering shrubs all year long but the best time is spring and early summer when the azaleas bloom in a variety of colors. Also, the many rhododendrons, which are closely related to the azalea, occasionally could be seen. Every so often, there were topiary plantings of animals hewn out of boxwoods. I returned to the hotel for an early night's sleep. I expect to go to Washuzan Hill the next day to view the many small islands of the Inland Sea. Washuzan is an eagle-shaped plateau with a grand view, which is one of the most enchanting in the Inland Sea.

After a filling American breakfast of toast, fried eggs and tea, I started out the next morning. I took the JR Sanyo line train at Kurashiki station one stop to Nakasho station where I got a taxicab to take me to the Hayashima station of the JR Seto-Ohashi line. I took this train to Kojima station. From the JR Kojima station, I took the Shimodem bus for Washuzan for 25 minutes and got off at the terminal. The island-studded beauty of the Inland Sea has inspired traveling poets and storytellers for centuries; the panoramic view from Washuzan is especially noteworthy for the harmony achieved between the staccato of the islands and the legato of the placid blue waters of the National Park. The islands are like a ribbon starting with Kamachima Island, Matsushima Island, Hitsuishi Island, Iwakuro Island, Kyoshima Island, Yoshima Island, Wasashima Island, Mitsugo Island thence to Sakaide City laid out in a long row. I was watching this magnificent scene before me with a polyphemic eye.

It's one thing to see – most of us are lucky enough to be anatomically endowed with two eyes (Sanskrit *akshi*), from which derives the special sense of vision, when all is working right. But vision in and of itself is a passive process, which is to say you don't have to think about it or do anything in order to see; it's automatic. Thus, all that vision allows us to do is take passive, instantaneous "snapshots" of our environment. However, just as it's one thing to hear, passively, but an entirely different thing to listen, actively, so too is seeing, passively, one thing but observing actively, something entirely different.

From the Latin prefix *ob-*, meaning "over" and *servare,* meaning, "to watch", to observe is "to watch over" in the sense of "seeing", passively, with deliberate intent of noticing and reacting, actively. In observing the line of islands in the Inland Sea, I became actively engaged in the visual process, investing the psychic energy required to be consciously aware of the significance of what I "see" as opposed to just passively taking things in through the sense of vision. The images created in my mind reminded me of paintings by Monet and Thomas Cole with their misty, ephemeral quality.

After a long day, I returned to Kurashiki station and decided to have a late lunch or perhaps an early dinner, whatever. I found a lovely small restaurant just outside the station. After perusing the menu, I ordered pickled Mamakari fish and a bowl of *gohan* (boiled rice). The fish was delicious and was sufficient when supplemented by the rice. I ordered a second bowl of rice, which I dressed with the sauce of the fish. I left the restaurant and passed slowly by a storefront with a sign painted in Japanese characters, *KAMI-SUKI-YA,* which I subsequently found out meant PAPER MAKER SHOP. Being curious, I went in and tried conversing with the proprietor, who spoke no English. In my broken Japanese and by showing him my sketchpad we were able to understand each other. I bought a few packages of *bitchu washi* Japanese paper. Japanese hand made paper, known as *washi,* often mistakenly called "rice" paper in the U.S., is an art, which is appreciated all over the world. It comes in many textures and weights and is used by artists, craftsmen and calligraphers.

The store next door was a greengrocer *(yaoya)* where I was able to purchase two bunches of Muscat grapes, a specialty of the region. I requested of the store- keeper – *"nagasu"*, which means – *to wash away.* The greengrocer exploded in laughter but obviously understood me and hurried away with the two bunches of grapes returning with them wrapped in tissue paper. I paid him with a bow and many thanks – *domo arigato.* I left the store while munching the sweet grapes as I strolled along. Fruit in Japan is really beautiful, particularly peaches and melons which are sold as expensive gifts. I then returned to the hotel and prepared for my trip to Okayama the next day.

VI

The next day I took the JR Sanyo Line for the short trip to Okayama and made my way to the Hotel Okayama Kokusai in the Higashiyama district. Okayama City developed during the Edo Period (1603-1876) as a powerful castle town. But today is the political, economic, cultural, and transportation center of Okayama Prefecture. The city is known throughout Japan for its splendid gardens.

After getting settled, I was anxious to visit the renowned Korakuen Park. Korakuen Park covers about 22 acres and is very close to the downtown area so I was able to take the Higashiyama street car from my hotel and then a short walk. Korakuen Park is one of the three most beautiful parks in Japan; the other two being Kairakuen in Mito and Kenrokuen in Kanazawa. Korakuen was laid out some 290 years ago (1686) by the feudal lord, Tsunamasa Ikeda. Every technique of the Enshu School of landscape gardening is employed in this bright and spacious "strolling garden". All the essentials of a traditional Japanese garden are present, large and small ponds, streams, hills and islands, paths winding between flowering shrubs, tea pavilions, groves, even a rice field. The large expanse of open lawn is unusual and is much admired.

Looming beyond the carefully manicured grounds of Korakuen, Okayama Castle stands out among Japan's medieval castles for its striking black exterior, for which it is known as *U Jo* or the "Crow Castle". After walking through Korakuen Park and inspecting Okayama Castle, I walked to the Nishigawa Greenway Canal. The canal is lined with numerous varieties of flowers and shade trees. This peaceful canal in the heart of the city, is a refreshing haven enjoyed by all who walk alongside. I saw many colorful carp (*koi*) swimming slowly upstream against the gentle current. But most striking were the beds of red and yellow tulips giving me the second impression of Amsterdam after Kurashiki.

I then walked to Okayama station and took the Tsuyama line to Handayama Botanical Garden. This garden is on a hillside over-looking Okayama City; a spectacular view. There are over 3200 species of plants, including a wonderful collection of plum trees, cherry trees, azaleas, and rhododendrons. Established in 1964, this expansive botanical garden utilizes a local reservoir and therefore is in bloom throughout the year.

Next I took the JR Tsuyama line back towards Okayama station, changed for the Kibi line, and got off at Natsukawa station for the long walk to the RSK Rose Garden. There are 150 varieties of roses, numbering some 70,000 plants, blooming one after the other from May to November in this garden. What a sight! Part of the rose garden is a lawn plaza where I relaxed on a bench and watched folk dancing in progress.

By now I was tired and hungry. I found a small restaurant front-ing route 2 near the rose garden and decided to go in. I ordered a pot of Uji green tea as I studied the menu. I found the same fish I had in Kurashiki – Mamakari – and learned from the waitress that it is a fish only found in the Inland Sea and that is why it is so prevalent in the towns bordering the Inland Sea.

I ordered Mamakari Zushi (made with boiled rice and vinegar) and sat back to enjoy it. After eating I needed something sweet in my mouth to overcome the vinegary aftertaste, so for dessert I had a plate of mixed fruits. Due to its warm and rather dry climate, Okaya-ma, the "Fruit Kingdom", produces a variety of delicious fruits: Muscat grapes, honeydew melons, and white peaches. Japanese confections are an important part of a meal. Okayama's contribution *kibidango* is a dumpling made of rice, starch syrup, and sugar. It was delicious.

After I left the restaurant, I came upon a store that sold tradi-tional Bizen Ware. Bizen Ware is a type of china originally from Bizen-cho in Okayama Prefecture. An unglazed pottery, it is famous for its solidity and quiet elegance. I bought a large tea mug, which I intend using as a pencil holder when I get home. I returned to my hotel to rest and have a hot bath to soak away my weary bones.

Being a museum crawler, I went the next day by train to the Bizen Osafune Museum near Imbe station, which was described to me by the proprietor of the Bizen Ware store yesterday. Iron from the northern mountain region made Bizen an important center of sword craftsmanship as early as the 8th century. The Kamakura (1192-1333) and Muromachi (1338-1573) Periods were marked by great battles throughout the land and the prevailing spirit of *Bushido* – the way of the Samurai – brought prosperity to this region.

In addition to demonstrations of traditional sword making, I was able to view these beautiful art treasures as well as earthenware and stone tools discovered nearby. I was anxious to see the Shizutani School built by Lord Ikeda in 1670 during the Edo Period. Shizutani School is nestled in a peaceful vale northeast of Bizen City. It was the first institution open to all citizens regardless of class or social rank. The school enclosed by a superbly crafted stone wall and with reddish-brown Bizen Ware roof tiles and stark white walls, contrasts splendidly with the natural beauty of the surrounding area.Oh dear, another long, vexing day.

VII

Once again on leaving Okayama I took the JR Yunagi train at 9:13 in the morning for a ½ hour ride to Uno, the port where I could get a JR Ferry for the one hour trip to Takamatsu on the island of Shikoku facing the Inland Sea. The ferry arrived in Takamatsu 10 minutes later with a load of cars and people. While on board, I noticed three Western boys dressed in white shirts and ties. This was very unusual because the weather was extremely hot. Obviously, they were not tourists. But what and who were they?

I approached them with a greeting and a question, "Aren't you fellows warm dressed with ties?" One fellow answered, "We are Mormon missionaries and we dress this way out of respect for our flock.

I was startled never having seen a missionary before.

"Mormons, eh? Tell me more."

"Well, Central to Mormon belief is the Restoration: the Churches have apostatized, but true Christianity has been restored by Joseph Smith. According to Smith, God is self made – only matter being eternal. Entrance to Christ's kingdom is by repentance. We are helping to spread our movement under a strong missionary imperative all over the world.

I exclaimed forcefully," But most Japanese are either Buddhists or Shintoists, some are both. That is their religion. Why do they need conversion?"

He looked at me with a steady gaze, "Because unless they convert they will be doomed to Hell."

I looked at him with moist eyes and said in an easy, graceful manner, "God may save all but human rescue is only for a few."

He raised his eyebrows producing frown lines along his forehead and said nothing so I continued, "I myself am heaven and hell, is a Buddhist adage."

I saw myself getting upset because to me persuasive conversion has always been anathema for as long as I can remember. I bade them goodbye and took my leave. I proceeded on my way to the hotel Takamatsu is a familiar castle town renowned as the land, sea and air gateway to Shikoku. I was anxious to see it all. After registering in the hotel, I made my way to Tamamo Park in which was located Takamatsu Castle. Takamatsu Castle is constructed with a unique design – three sides of the castle are surrounded by moats filled with seawater. A park on the castle grounds adds a tranquil atmosphere, despite its proximity to Takamatsu station at the city center. I particularly enjoyed one attraction of special interest, *tsukimiyagura*, a watchtower for detecting enemy boats. I enjoyed the sea view of the Inland Sea while listening to the voices of history on the wind.

The area around JR Takamatsu station is of special interest, because there are plans for construction to integrate the harbor and urban functions, but that is a long time away. Right now, the area is a sort of plaza for busses.

Since the day was still early and the sun was high, I decided to visit Ritsurin Park. By now my readers must know of my love for gardens. Ritsurin Park was the garden of a feudal lord. Its six ponds and thirteen miniature mountains are arranged in front of a green mountain known as *Shiunzan*. The park was built in the Edo Period, and was enlarged several times during the more than 100 years since the *Kanei* Era (around 1625). It is a nationally designated place of scenic beauty.

I then took the train for the short ride along the shoreline of the Inland Sea to Marugame so that I could see Nakatsu-Bansho Park. The second feudal lord of Marugame Castle built this park in 1688. The pond at the center of the park is shaped to resemble Lake Biwa near Kyoto. Some of the islands arranged in the pond have been given elegant names such as "Snow" and "Moon". The park also houses Marugame Art Gallery, which features exhibits of paintings by Millet and Corot as well as Hina dolls from the Edo Period. I am always stunned by the presence of so much Western art in Japanese museums.

Marugame Castle is situated on a flattop mountain. It is surrounded by a beautiful curved stonewall known as a "fan-shaped slope". This castle is also renowned for its cherry blossoms in spring. It is only a 15-minute walk from the JR Marugame Station. By this time I was very hungry not having eaten all day. I sought out a restaurant near the station.

When I entered the restaurant, the hostess greeted me with a deep bow and whispered words. I removed my shoes and was led to a small, low table and was immediately served a hot mug of green tea. I ordered *Tai-men* from the picture menu. The Tai (sea bream) was caught that morning at Ehime Prefecture. Tai-men is a dish comprising an entire fish placed over *somen* (thin noodles) and cooked. Apparently, Tai-men is a very popular dish sometimes cooked over rice. I preferred the noodles since I am fascinated by the various styles of Japanese noodles.

I returned to Takamatsu late in the day and decided to relax at the hotel. A lovely garden and an expansive lawn surround the hotel. The weather was pleasantly warm and I was induced to sit in one of the lawn chairs where after a few minutes I dozed off. I was awakened by the *Obasan* (hotel mistress) who brought me a tray of tea and Japanese cookies. I must confess that Japanese baked goods are not to my liking, perhaps because they are made with rice flour. Nevertheless, I enjoyed the tea and was touched by her kindness.

The next day, I took the JR train to Koto-den Yashima station. It was only a five-minute walk to the Shikoku Folklore House Museum. This museum covers an area of about 50,000 square yards. It features traditional houses from various regions of Shikoku. Most of the houses are so valuable they have been designated important National cultural properties. I really felt I was thrust back in time while exploring these houses and walking the streets.

At the conclusion of my visit to the Shikoku Houses Museum, I returned to the Takamatsu station and decided to sit and gawk at the people in the plaza for a while. I found a bench partially occupied by a well-dressed gentleman.

"Konnichiwa (good day)," I greeted him. "Konnichiwa," he answered.

"My name is Shansky Albert", I said in English hoping he would understand me. To my surprise, he answered in perfect English, "My name is HiranoYuichi."

We both laughed as he continued, "I am waiting here for my wife who is due here soon after an eleven hour bus trip from Tokyo."

"You speak English very well. Where did you learn it?" I queried.

He answered with a certain pride," I spent some years in Wilmette, Illinois.

"Wilmette, Illinois?"

"Yes, I was a student at the Bahai Temple there."

"Bahai Temple?"

"Yes. I am in charge of the Bahai Temple here on Kasuga-cho in Takamatsu."

For the want of anything better to say I blurted out, "How interesting. Tell me about the Bahai Faith. Is it like Buddhism?"

He laughed loudly while saying mirthfully, "No. no. not at all. Let me tell you something about the Bahai Faith."

"The Bahai Faith is a religion founded by Baha-ullah in the 1860s. The religion preaches a message of global socio-religious reform. The religion started in Iran but expanded beyond the social and conceptual universe of Iranian Shi'ism, attracting converts from elsewhere. Bahais from these other areas now constitute the majority of the world's five million Bahais. We are regarded as heretics by Islamic authorities and have been subject to persecution."

"Do you believe in a God?"

"Bahai is monotheistic, but God is regarded as in essence completely transcendent and unknowable."

"Do you engage in missionary activity or conversions?"

"No, we do not. Religious life centers on various individual acts of devotion such as daily obligatory prayer and moral self-accounting."

"I see. That is very interesting. Are your members here from the local Japanese people?"

"Yes, of course. Most have been born as Buddhists and many practice both religions."

Just then a large transport bus pulled into the plaza and Hirano got up in anticipation. His wife alighted from the bus and I was somewhat startled to see that she was a Western woman. He introduced her to me and I learned she was American. I assumed they met when he lived in Evanston, Illinois. They both said goodbye and drove off leaving me alone to ponder on the presence of Bahai in Japan.

The next day I took the JR train to Tadotsu following the beautiful shoreline of the Inland Sea, a never tiring view. There I changed for a train to Zentzuji. Zentuji Temple is known as the 75th amulet site of Japan's famed pilgrimage of the 88 Sacred Temples of Shikoku. This temple dates back to the year 813 and took about six years to build. It comprises the Eastern Hall with its Southern Great Gate and a five-storied pagoda, and the Western Hall with a back room. It is believed that Kobo Daishi, the propagator of these 88 temples circling Shikoku, was born there. I could see a group of pilgrims in their white uniforms milling about the grounds. It reminded me of the Ishite Temple that I visited with Ken. I returned to Takamatsu in preparation for leaving the next day. I went to the Kansai Kisen Steamship Company office in Takamatsu to make arrangements for the trip to Osaka.

VIII

Takamatsu to Osaka by the Kansai Kisen Steamship, takes about 5 hours, leaving at 7:30 in the morning. On this modest little ship, I found my accommodation limited to a cushioned chair and free cups of tea, but I did enjoy meeting the people on board. In particular, I made friends with a young backpacking student who said, in rather good English, that he would lead me to the Loop Line train after debarking since he was going that way to meet his girlfriend. I was planning on staying at the Hotel Osaka International.

I went on deck to view the disappearing Inland Sea as the boat sailed into open water heading toward Osaka Bay and the Kansai region. I became a little sad as I thought about my recent adventures on the Inland Sea. I vowed silently to return someday.

Suddenly, I felt a hand on my shoulder. I turned around to find the young student greeting me, "What is your name? My name is Kamikawa Goku. My first name, Goku, means five lakes."

I immediately responded with an extended hand, "My name is Shansky Albert. You may call me Al."

He answered in a strident, shrill voice, "Oh no Shansky-san that would be impolite."

"Ok. Do you live in Osaka?"

"No, I live in Takamatsu but I go to school in Osaka at Osaka University. I take the Kansai steamship back and forth quite frequently."

"Is that so? What are you studying in school?'

He seemed embarrassed as his face reddened in response, "I am studying Buddhism."

I was taken aback momentarily but slowly replied, "I am interested in Buddhism. I understand there are many concepts in Buddhism. Which concept of Buddhism gives you the most attention? What I mean is which concept due you focus on most?"

He answered without hesitation, "Dependent Origination is a key concept. I suppose it has the most meaning for me."

I queried, "What is Dependent Origination?"

He paused and began stammering, "Dependent Origination is known in Sanskrit as *paticca-samuppada*. It is sometimes called interdependent arising."

He paused again but continued, "It states that all physical and mental manifestations which constitute individual appearances are interdependent and condition or affect one another, in a constant process of arising (*samudaya*) and ceasing to be (*nirodha*). Every appearance is connected to, and, depends on, some other appearance: nothing, except the absolute, non interactive state of Nirvana can escape its connectedness to some other manifestation, so that all unravels as surely as it is knitted together."

I was astonished by his answer and being somewhat overwhelmed felt impelled to comment. "Well that seems logical. You mean that when two people meet, such as us, they become modified by the influence on each other."

He looked at me prodigiously as if he was affected with astonishment as he said, "In a sense that's true. But it is more than that."

I was excited by something strange and not well understood. I noticed he was staring at me putatively with naïve eyes. Nothing more was said.

After a while the boat entered Osaka Bay. I am looking forward to exploring this large and forbidding city of 3 million inhabitants. Central Osaka is predominantly a business district. The JR Kanjo-sen (Loop Line) circles the city center. Osaka station the primary train station for the city, is at the north end of this loop. This is where my hotel was located.

Goku and I debarked with the other passengers scurrying down the gangplank. We headed for the Nankai Hankai Line, which would eventually change to the JR Kanto-sen Line (Loop Line). Goku walked so fast I found myself unable to keep up with him while carrying my bag by the shoulder strap so I waved him off with a fond farewell. I eventually got off at the JR Osaka station and headed for my hotel after some judicious direction inquiries. Not being tired, I decided to begin my explorations after registering in the hotel.

I started my exploration of Osaka with the city's major landmark, *Osaka-jo*, the castle that Hideyoshi Toyotomi built in the late 16th century. I reached it by taking the Loop Line from Osaka station to Osaka-jo Koen station, from which it's a 10-minute walk, uphill through the park. The castle was an amazing formidable structure with a show of the battle that took place there. I could almost see the soldiers rushing up each level with drawn swords, causing mayhem, death and destruction on their way up to the top floors.

Outside the castle there was an exhibit of bonsai plants in progress. Some were so intriguing as to make one believe they were miniature villages. I wanted to see the ceramics exhibits of the Municipal Art Museum of Asian Ceramics, which is on the eastern end of Naka-no-shima, the island in Naka-no-shima Koen. To get there I had to walk northeast for 5 minutes to Kyobashi station and take the Keihan Line to the Yodoya-bashi stop. The museum was a five-minute walk away. I never saw so many different types of ceramic artifacts in one place. There were pots, vases, ewers, cups and dishes, decorated in many different colorful styles. It was a really enjoyable place and I particularly loved the Imari Ware and the special case of Noritake crockery. But now I was getting tired and decided to call it a day and return to my hotel.

It was a 15-minute walk up to the city's Umeda district and the JR Osaka station. There I found a small inviting restaurant and ordered Osaka-Zushi, flavored with a soy sauce that is lighter in color, milder in flavor and saltier in content than soy sauce used in Tokyo. The Osaka sushi is made in wooden molds and has a distinctive square shape. I had this with my ubiquitous pot of green tea (ryoku-cha). After resting for an hour in my hotel room I decide to attend a performance at the Puppet Theater.

Osaka is the home of Bunraku (puppet drama), which originated during the Heian Period (794-1192). In the late 17th and 18th centuries the genius of local playwright Chikamatsu distilled Bunraku as an art form. Bunraku puppets are about two- thirds human size. Three puppeteers move the puppets, and they are completely visible to the audience despite wearing black uniforms. I saw a play, which dealt with a theme of tragic love at the National Bunraku Theater; the story was chanted in song by a *joruri*, who was accompanied by ballad music played on a three-stringed instrument known as a shamisen. Although I did not understand the words, the tone of the music set an appropriate mood of pathos. I really enjoyed the Bunraku performance. Perhaps tomorrow I shall attend a Kabuki performance at the Shochiku-za Kabuki Theater in the Dotombori area. I remember how much I enjoyed Kabuki at the Kabuki-za in Tokyo.

The next day I headed for Sumiyoshi Taisha, one of three most famous Shinto shrines in Japan built in the 8th century. This required taking the Loop Line to Tennoji station and changing for the Nankai Hankai Line. But while at Tennoji station I thought it wise to visit nearby Shitennoji on the way. Shitennoji Temple is the oldest Buddhist temple in Japan. While there I bought a poster of the temple to hang in my house when I get home.

I continued to Sumiyoshi Taisha. Sumiyoshi Taisha has a Japanese cypress structure that's painted vermilion. Sumiyoshi is also the name given to this Shinto style of architecture. Sumiyoshi Taisha honors the goddess of sea voyages, Sumiyoshi, and, according to legend, was founded by Empress Jingu in 211 to express her gratitude for her safe return from a voyage to Korea. On the shrine's grounds are many stone lanterns donated by sailors and ship owners as dedications to Sumiyoshi and other Shinto deities that guard the voyages of seafarers. I noticed the arched bridge, which was given by Yodogimi, the consort of Hidayoshi Toyotomi, who bore him a son.

Afterwards I headed back on the Loop Line to Senri Expo Park and its museums, the National Museum of Ethnology which contains Ainu artifacts and the Japan Folk Art Museum. These museums gave me inkling into Japan's ancient past. I spent the remainder of the day there, but it was another long day. I headed back to Osaka station for the restaurant in which I ate yesterday. I ordered the oko-nomiyaki, which are grilled pancakes filled with cabbage, mountain yams, pork, shrimp, and other ingredients. I remember how much I enjoyed it when Kim introduced me to this lovely delicacy in Hiro-shima. I expect to go to Dotombori to see a Kabuki play this eve-ning. At the end of the day Dotombori-dori (street) is the place to go for dinner and nightlife.

I was told by the front desk of the hotel to look for *toyoyaki*, which are grilled cooked dumplings with bits of octopus, green on-ions, and ginger smothered in a delicious sauce, when I get there. Street vendors along Dotombori-dori sell this tasty snack. I love finger food like Spanish tapas and nothing is more enjoyable than eating while walking on the street, especially if others are doing the same.

This time I would have to take the subway from Kita-Shinchi to Namba and walk north two blocks. The good life of Dotombori's restaurants and bars lures flocks of Osakans here to forget their daily toils. The street – a virtual feast for neonophiles – runs alongside Dotombori-gawa (river), and it's the place to stroll in the evening for a glimpse of Osaka nightlife.

At the Kabuki Theater there was a revolving stage and two trap lifts. The larger one is used for quick changes in stage props. The smaller one is for lifting actors up to floor level. Equally fascinating are the sets of sliding *shoji* (screens) used to adjust the amount of daylight filtering onto the stage.

Shochiku Kabuki is one of two wealthiest and most powerful theatrical organizations in Japan. Twin brothers founded it in 1902 in Kyoto. In 1910, one went to Tokyo where eventually he man-aged the Kabuki-za. The other brother remained in the Kamigata area eventually moving to Osaka after World War II.

For the first time, I experienced Japanese Kabuki in all of its resplendent authenticity with a representation of *Natsumatsuri, Na-*

niwa Kagami, starring Nakamura Kankuro V, one of Japan's most famous Kabuki actors. In keeping with the production's genuine spirit there is a *hanamichi* (a walkway extending down the center of the theater). I was lucky to be able to get a cushioned seat at the intersection of the walkway and the main stage.

The legendary Nakamura Kankuro V and fellow actors performed this version of *Natsumatsuri Naniwa Kagami,* a tale of chivalrous men and their struggles to balance love, responsibility, and marital devotion. Since the 17th century, Nakamura Kankuro V's family has been synonymous with the world of Kabuki, a 400-year-old art form passed from one generation to the next.

The next day Ichikawa Danjuro will play the dashing Sukeroku in the popular and colorful "Sukeroku Yukari No Edo Zakura" which is one of four matinee numbers, a very long program. So I decided to come back the next day for the performance. I arrived at 10:00 am to stand in line to buy tickets for the all day performance. While standing in line I was aware that someone behind me was trying to gain my attention. I turned to see a middle aged woman who spoke to me in passable English, "Are you waiting to buy a ticket?" I answered forthrightly, "Yes, I am." She spoke again while holding up a ticket in her hand. "This ticket is my husband's but he could not come. You may have it." I was startled at this kindness, "Well, at least, let me pay you for it." "Oh, no" she said. "It is my pleasure to give it to you" I took the ticket and began a conversation with her. Her name is Yuko Yamaguchi. We sat together in extremely wonderful seats. The theater was sold out.

The first play is a forte of the Ichikawa family of actors.

Sukeroku is in fact Soga Goro of the famous Soga brothers seeking revenge against their father's killer. He frequently visits the Miuraya in the Yoshiwara licensed quarters (pleasure quarter) of Edo (former Tokyo). His lover there is a courtesan Agemaki, played by Nakamura Jakuemon. His purpose is to find the missing treasure sword Tomokirimaru.

Ikyu, a bewhiskered former samurai, seeks Agemaki's favors. She spurns him for she is in love with Sukeroku. The dandy appears and deliberately insults Ikyu in the hope that the old man will draw his sword in anger. Sukeroku suspects that the old man's sword is indeed the missing one. Later, Ikyu does draw the sword which Sukeroku instantly recognizes to be Tomokirimaru.

The second number on the program was the famous period work "Ichi No Tani Futabagunki" concerning the Genji clan warrior Kumagai Jiro Naozane.

The scene is called "Kumagai Jinya" or Kumagai's camp in the field. Kumagai's wife visits the camp, concerned about their son Kojiro in his first battle. Also visiting is Fuji-no-kata, mother of Atsumori of the rival Heike clan. She was a lady-in-waiting to the emperor who had sired Atsumori. She had heard that Kumagai had killed her son on the battlefield and thus had come to seek vengeance. Kumagai relates the battle to the two women.

The ritual of "kubijikken" follows to verify that the severed head is truly that of the person claimed to have been killed. Lord Minamoto Yoshitsune inspects the head that is brought in. It is that of Kumagai's son Kojiro, not Atsumori's. Yoshitsune gives no hint of a sign that he knows there has been a substitution. Indebted to Atsumori's mother in the past, Kumagai had sacrificed his own son.

Sagami and Fuji-no-kata pretend the head is Atsumori's. Realizing the cruelty and transience of the warrior's life, Kumagai decides to enter the Buddhist priesthood.

The third matinee piece is "Dewa-no-kami to Senhime" Osaka castle falls. Sakazaki Dewa-no-kami rescues the princess Senhime from the flames. Her grandfather the shogun Tokugawa Ieyasu had promised to give the princess to Dewa-no-kami if he saved her. The brave warrior stops Senhime when she tries to kill herself upon learning that her husband Hideyori had died in battle. Dewa-no-kami's feeling for the princess mounts. But she cannot do anything about it. A warrior comes to escort her and she is struck by his resemblance to her late husband. Danjuro played Dewa-no-kami.

The fourth and final matinee number is "Satsuki Yami Utsunoya Toge" with Onoe Kikugoro playing the dual roles of Bunya the blind masseuse and Jinzo the scoundrel. The Edo sake shop keeper Jyubei, played by Danjuro, is in need of money to help his former master, He cannot raise the money. He saves the masseur Bunya from the scoundrel Jinzo at an inn. The two leave the inn before dawn and come to the Utsunoya Toge mountain pass. Jyubei learns that Bunya has a large amount of money on his person. Steeling his heart, Jyubei kills Bunya and takes the money. Jinzo, who witnesses the scene, tries to blackmail Jyubei. Kikugoro does a quick change to play the roles of the frail masseuse and the scoundrel.

The matinee started at 11 am and continued all day, with a break for lunch, until 5:30 pm.I purchased two bentos (box lunches) with two glasses of cold tea at the commissary for lunch with Yuko Yamaguchi. She thanked me and we continued talking about the performances. I admitted that my favorite actor was Danjuro to which she agreed. After the performance I walked Yuko to the train and bid her a fond farewell.

The unusual thing about Kabuki is the staging and the costumes. It is all so real with the ability to thrust one back to a bygone era. The stories, as can be seen, are all about unrequited love, revenge, lust and other human foibles – much like Shakespeare. I had purchased a "libretto" so that I could follow the action of the stories.

Oh, what joy? I love Kabuki.

IX

The Inland Sea, according to geologists, is the happy creation of a titanic upheaval that created the Kibi plateau, which is today Okayama Prefecture, and wrenched Kyushu and Shikoku and 3000 smaller islands apart from Honshu.

In the early days of Japanese history, the ancient culture of continental Asia was first introduced into Kyushu and then spread through the great interior artery of the Inland Sea over the rest of the country.

The area today represents the true Japan – the Japan of ancient customs, crafts, and superlative scenery, and the Japan of modern industries, crowds, and commerce. Its waters teem with fish, and the land blossoms with orchards, vegetable plantations, and tiers of paddy fields that rise like giant staircases up the sides of the hilly slopes that flank the shores of the sea. Several centuries ago, when a Chinese visitor saw how the paddy fields had been hewn from the mountainsides around the Inland Sea he remarked, "Here they build their gardens to the very gates of heaven!" Here too are shipbuilding yards, steel plants, petroleum refineries, and other great industrial facilities.

The three thousand islands of the Inland Sea offer an infinite variety of sights, moods and sounds. Their mood changes in every season. They offer something for everyone and well deserve leisurely exploration.

X

Finally, it was time to leave Osaka. The next day, I took the PanAm flight 830 from Osaka airport to Narita airport in Tokyo at 4:50 in the afternoon to arrive at 6:05 in the later afternoon. I checked in at the New Otani Hotel. It was my intention to remain at least a day to explore Chichibu.

The next morning I walked from the New Otani Hotel to the Akasaka Mitsuke Station on the Marunouchi Line and traveled to the Ikebukuro Station. From there I went to the Seibu Railroad terminus and took the Red Arrow Express at 7:00 am to the Seibu Chichibu Station, a ninety minute ride. I arrived at 9:00 am. I decide last night to visit Temples 10 through 18 on the advice of the tour desk in the lobby of the hotel. Indeed, they were able to procure round trip rail tickets for me since all seats on the train are reserved.

When I reached the Seibu Chichibu Station, I approached a taxi driver, saying to him, *"Gaijin desu. Juban kudasai."* (I am a foreigner. Temple 10 please.) The taxi driver was an amiable fellow who wore spectacles with Coke-bottle lenses which made his eyes bulge alarmingly. He had an enormous small-toothed smile. He responded, "Hai, hai," as he opened the door automatically. I got in and we traveled silently to Temple 10 and stopped at a large Jizo statue on a high pedestal. Jizo is the protector of children and travelers. I walked up the steep stone stairway behind the statue and walked through the weathered roofed gate of Temple 10, Daiji-ji.

Daiji-ji is a quiet but attractive temple that enjoys enthusiastic support from the neighborhood. The local people sew bibs for the Jizo statue and care for the temple. The simple Zen-style building has sliding doors covered with senja-fuda, origami figures, sutras written on paper, and many other small items donated by pilgrims. Inside is a beautifully carved altar, where lighted candles are offered.

On both sides of the altar hang silk banners decorated with gold and silver phoenixes. A gently worn, carved figure near the doors on the left is a popular folk saint called Obinzuru-sama, derived from the legendary Indian saint Pindola. This saint is supposed to have saved many ill and suffering people with his medical knowledge and skill. Worshippers therefore rub the parts of the statue that correspond to their own ailments, praying for a cure. This rubbing makes the statue of Obinzuru-sama smooth and shining.

I bade goodbye to the Jizo and walked some distance to Hitsu-jiyama Park. I continued through the park and kept the hill on my right until I could see a stone torii and some white banners. The entrance to Temple 11, Joraku-ji is marked by a stone pillar to the left. From the entrance road, Chichibu City can be seen beyond a cement factory. The well-cared for Kannon Temple continues to withstand heavy pollution from the mundane world below.

A trail winds upward through many vermillion torii and tall cedars. The red wooden gates and banners near them are offerings to Inari, a popular folk god, a shrine to whom is located at the top of the hill. Continuing uphill, I reached a small shrine. A hiking path leads in the direction of the Chichibu Folk Museum. I did not go there because it was in the opposite direction from that of the next temple.

Leaving Temple 11, I backtracked, crossing a small stream and continued straight ahead. I enjoyed a slight detour through Hitsuji-yama. A winding driveway ascends to the top of the hill. Just before the summit is a pond with a water wheel. It was built in memory of Wakayama Bokusui, a poet who visited Chichibu in the early twentieth century when the area was humming with the silk industry. He composed a *waka*, a thirty-one syllable poem, describing the neighborhood. It has been inscribed on a stone by the pond.

At the top of the hill, I walked along the densely wooded side road, past cherry trees. A little further I could see the red torii, where I found a blue and white sign proclaiming "Antioch Park" reflecting a relationship between Chichibu City and Antioch, California. I took the short path which was a pleasantly wooded walk to the next temple. At the bottom of the hill I passed a small cemetery and then went under the railway underpass. A beautifully plastered white wall can be seen, behind which is Temple 12.

I continued straight passing by a charming Jizo. I noticed the sun, moon, and old characters on the stone marker to the left of the Jizo. Around the corner is the ryokan Hiyoshi but I had no intention of spending the night. So I kept walking until I arrived at Temple 12. Entering through a charming two-story wooden gate, I walked into the well-tended compound of Temple 12, Nosaka-ji. This temple basks in the sunshine, as well as in the favor of its worshippers. The large main building is very impressive. The monk's living quarters is busy with people in animated conversation. Some of the stone monuments in the compound are very interesting, and the walls of the main building are decorated with wooden figures depicting twenty-five bodhisattvas floating on clouds.

A temple legend tells of Kannon rescuing a traveler from bandits. Once a merchant from Kai (Yamanashi Prefecture) happened to pass the area and was assaulted by a group of armed robbers, who stripped him of his clothes and threatened to kill him. In despair the merchant prayed frantically to Kannon. Suddenly strong beams of light flashed from his amulet case and struck the eyes of the robbers. Dazzled by the light they all fled, except for the leader. Awe-struck and penitent, he vowed to become a follower of Kannon. Several years later, the merchant came back and found the former bandit living in a shack and dedicated to his religious discipline. Very impressed, the merchant had a temple built for him at the site, which made the founding of Nosaka-ji. A dazzling light is often emblematic of the power of Kannon.

Leaving Nosaka-ji, I walked straight past several buildings where there is an excellent soba noodle restaurant, Koike, in a simply but beautifully decorated building. I stopped here to have an early lunch. I love soba noodles and had two helpings, *Oishi* (delicious). I left the restaurant and headed for the Seibu Chichibu Station. Some interesting shops are located conveniently near the station. The shopping area right at the station has noodle shops and *yakatori* (skewered, grilled chicken) restaurants, both convenient for snacks. A stall is set up at the entrance of the shopping area to sell country-style dumplings called *Oyaki*. The dumplings have several kinds of vegetable fillings; my favorites are *nasu* (eggplant) and *yasai* (mixed vegetables). At the far end of the passageway is a bamboo-basket shop; behind is a fabric shop, where a loom is set up to demonstrate the weaving of a silk textile called *meisen*, which was a popular kimono material for women's daily wear and a special product of Chichibu.

I crossed the railroad tracks and walked straight ahead until I came to a solid wooden gate. I entered Temple 13, Jigan-ji. I immediately saw the Kannon hall in front of me. There was a large building on the left which was the monk's quarters. A kindergarten is attached to the temple, and the spacious compound was crowded with children. The walls and pillars of the Kannon hall are elaborately carved. Though colors have faded over the years, the diverse designs reflect the pride of worshippers, who renovated it at the turn of the century.

A small temple to the right of the Kannon hall is dedicated to Yakushi, a Buddhist god of medicine. Worship of this temple god, popularly called Ame Yakushi, is efficacious for treating ailments. The building to the right with thick walls is a warehouse for precious sutras, some dating from the seventh century, stored in a hexagonal shelf around the building's central pillar. The brightly painted statues on the right depict the thirteen saints who allegedly, founded the pilgrimages in Chichibu in the tenth century. The group is a hodge-podge of Buddhist saints, Shinto gods, former emperors, mountain ascetics, and folk figures, all of whom supposedly came from nether world to Chichibu to pray on behalf of the local people for Kannon's blessings. The course of the pilgrimage subsequently became popular for people seeking salvation. Grouping together these characters representing various beliefs is an example of the Japanese penchant for diversity and eclecticism.

62

I left the temple by the far rear gate behind the Kannon hall and walked to Temple 14, Imamiya-bo. The street is lined with shops. On the right is an antique shop, Ozeki, which had some very interesting ancient things. Further along the street, around the corner from a Japanese sweets shop, is the restaurant Sushi Katsu, offering sushi, tempura and many other dishes, which are displayed in the front window. Still further along the street is a quiet coffee shop called Kawada. The walls of this small shop are also used as a gallery for local artists to show their works.

Further ahead the street intersects with a larger one called Chichibu Okan, the main street of Chichibu City. It bustled with people shopping and meandering. I crossed the main street and continued straight until I came to a small park, where a huge five-hundred year-old *keyaki* (zelkova) tree grows. Behind it is a small shrine, Imamiya-jinja. The shrine used to be an integral part of Temple 14, Imamiya-bo, two blocks further ahead.

Imamiya-bo thrived as a base of mountain asceticism in medieval and feudal times. However, when religious reforms were introduced by the Meiji government in the early 1870s, the mixed style of Shintoism and Buddhism was banned, and Imamiya-bo and Imamiya-jinja were separated. Traces of its past glory can be seen in the elegant style of its architecture, with its sophisticated roof lines, perhaps designated by a master carpenter of the late- Edo period.

The temple has preserved an eleventh-century wooden statue of celestial beauty, about a foot tall. The decorative motif of such graceful angels soaring on clouds, usually mounted on walls, was used in many temples to enhance the beauty of the principal deity. From this point I can spot in the distance the trees of the park I passed a while ago. So I walked through the park again and passed the five-hundred-year-old zelkova tree to return to the main street, Chichibu Okan. I passed a large supermarket called D-Mart but even though I was curious I didn't go in. Instead, I went into the bookstore next door called Miyamae Shoten. The store had a large collection of books on Chichibu. Unfortunately they were all in Japanese so I did not think it worth purchasing any even though some had very lovely pictures.

I left the bookstore and went directly across the street to a soba noodle restaurant called Tengu-ya. On entering I noticed it was small with many small tables. I sat down to have my second fill of soba noodles for the day. I really enjoy soba noodles. I left the small restaurant and went down a narrow lane. Continuing straight I came to a small tobacco shop where the road crosses a busier street called Banba-dori. I arrived at Chichibu-jinja and saw that Temple 15, Shorin-ji, lies just ahead.

The concrete building of Temple 15, Shorin-ji, appears strange at first sight. It was built in the style of a *kura* (store house), but fronted with a temple-style entrance, due to frequent fires in the nineteenth century. The original Temple 15 was called Zofuku-ji. It no longer exists, having been abolished at the time of the religious reforms that reduced Imamiya-bo. The solution to this problem was a merger with another temple, Shorin-ji, according that temple the position of Temple 15.

To the right of the Kannon hall is a wisteria arbor similar to one I have at home. From here Mt. Buko can be seen in the distance, clouds are suddenly rising and shrouding the top. I continued to Temple 16 by crossing the intersection. I decided to visit Chichibu-jinja on the way to temple 16, Saiko-ji.

I entered the concrete torii of Chichibu-jinja. Although the gate marks the present southwestern boundary of the compound, the shrine in former days was much larger, encompassing the area around Banba-dori and several blocks behind the shrine buildings. The precincts were once thickly forested with giant cedar, *hinoki*, and *keyaki*. Cutting them was strictly taboo for centuries. The large property was donated by Ieyasu, the first Shogun, in the sixteenth century.

I walked through the gate to the main building. One can see that income from the estate was generously spent in the construction of this building. Reflecting the dynamism and taste of the age of warring lords, numerous painted sculptures fill the panels of its walls and transoms. However, the motifs used – animals and characters of Japanese mythology – are not excessively ornate and balance well with the geometric contours of the building. The most famous figures, a dragon and tigers, are attributed to the master sculptor, Hidari Jingoro, who may be a legendary figure. Due to the damage suffered from a typhoon in 1966, the building was disassembled and restored to its original beauty in 1970. The architectural plan of the shrine is oriented toward Mt. Buko. Officially, the shrine is dedicated to three gods of Japanese mythology and to the late Prince Chichibu, although the origin of the shrine can likely be traced to the animistic worship of Mt. Buko. Throughout the history of Chichibu, the shrine has occupied an important place in the lives of the local residents.

A note on terminology: most Buddhist places of worship are called in Japanese tera, (or dera or ji), usually translated "temple." Some others are called do, meaning "hall." Shinto places of worship are usually jinja translated "shrine." Another useful term to know is torii, the double-tiered archway that marks the entrance to Shinto shrines.

I left the shrine compound by the side exit next to the red building, Kagura hall, and walked toward the big intersection with the traffic light. On the far left corner, is the Kato Modern Art Museum. On entering the museum I first passed by the lounge area with its handsome *keyaki* wood table and Isamu Noguchi lanterns hung from the ceiling. It reminded me of the time my wife and I visited Isamu Noguchi's workshop in Long Island City, New York, which is now a museum. I sat down for a moment to rest and take a breather. Looking at the Noguchi lanterns was not only enjoyable with their different shapes but quiet and restful.

Stepping into the first room I was surprised to find paintings and prints by Andrew Wyeth on the thick plastered walls of the building. The remainder of the collection includes oils and prints by Leonard Foujita, Amadeo Modigliani, Marc Chagall, and other members of the Ecole de Paris group. After leaving the museum I walked around the building to enjoy the view of the exterior walls, which resemble those of a castle.

The next temple is down the street several blocks. I walked to the crossing with the small triangular stone marker. From there I made a right turn to Temple 16, Saiko-ji. As I stepped into the temple compound, I faced a large main building, dating from the nineteenth century. The right section of the main building contains eighty-eight statues of various deities of the Buddhist pantheon, representing in miniature the course of the eighty-eight temples of the Henro pilgrimage on Shikoku Island. The miniature course was established in 1783, to pray for the souls following the devastating eruption of Mt. Asama that year.

I could not miss the gazebo-like hall in front of the main building. The pillars and the center of the altar are pitted with nail holes, from the old custom of nailing wooden votive tablets as proof of pilgrim's visits. The practice is now banned. The hall dates from the Edo period and is an interesting reminder of old customs. I backtracked to the crossing with the triangular marker and continued straight on the main street Chichibu-Okan. I had to endure walking on this busy street until I came to a black-and-white signboard indicating the approach to Temple 17. Jorin-ji.

At the end of the lane, I came to a simple Kannon hall with a belfry. The faded colors of its painted ceiling still retain some of its nineteenth century beauty. After leaving the temple, I found myself on the main street Chichibu-Okan once again. I came across a small shelter with a stone statue of a turtle inside it and a well beneath it. Both the turtle and the well are related to the legend of Myoken Bodhisattva who is a mysterious goddess believed to be the reincarnation of the seven stars in the Big Dipper constellation. I followed the local custom and splashed the turtle with the provided dipper. I continued walking until I reached Temple 18, Godo-ji.

Godo-ji or the Divine Gate Temple has lost much of its former charm. A legend has it that two *sakaki* trees (sacred evergreens) that grew here twined around each other to form a front gate. Old people in the neighborhood take turns with the chores of inscribing temple books, cleaning the Kannon hall and serving free tea to pilgrims.

This ended my Chichibu pilgrimage. Next I made my way to Seibu Chichibu Station by first calling the Marutsu taxi company. The yellow cab came to the temple's parking lot almost immediately. The taxi brought me to the station at 5:00 pm. The train was scheduled to leave at 5:15 pm. I was very tired after a day of walking and gawking. I had time, while on the train, to reflect on this pilgrimage which is a worship and reverence for Kannon.

No Buddhist deity in Japan has inspired such a wealth of artistic creation, religious tradition, and folk custom and belief as has Kannon (Kuan yin in Chinese, Avalokiteshvara in Sanskrit). The name is often translated Goddess of Mercy, but the deity may assume male or female form. In the Buddhist pantheon, Kannon is a Bodhisattva (in Japanese, *Bosatsu*), an enlightened being who has foregone Nirvana in order to remain on earth and help those who are suffering. This personification of infinite compassion, this Bodhisattva will render aid to all who invoke the name Kannon, which literally means "helper of cries."

I only managed to do a day walk (about eight miles) visiting only eight temples of the thirty four Kannon temples established in the eighteenth century. But this was my plan. I did not have enough time to do more as much as I would have wanted. I had to get home.

Harried by the pressure and competition of the modern urban lifestyle, people are turning to the warmth and comfort provided by the traditional faith in Kannon.

I arrived at the Ikebukuro Station tired and somewhat exhausted but aroused emotionally. I took the local train back to the Hotel New Otani and looked forward to a long, leisurely rest, a warm bath and a hearty meal. The next day I was to leave Japan for the long airplane trip home. I went directly to Narita Airport and took PanAm flight 800, leaving Narita at 7:15 in the evening, arriving at JFK airport at 6:45 in the evening.

AFTERWORD

The information in this story was supplemented by my personal visits to Japan and the experiences I garnered while there. The character Takahira Kenji, known as Ken in the story, is a real person with whom I have had some occasional contact but has now waned to my sorrow.

It might be worthwhile to mention that the boat trips Ken and I took in 1981 from Imabari to Oshima Island and then to Ikuchijima Island and finally to Mihara on the mainland was the only way to cross the Inland Sea at the time. Now they have a bridge or series of bridges linking six islands in the Inland Sea by ten bridges crossing the distance from Imabari on Shikoku to Onomichi on Honshu. This is called the Setouchi Shimanami Seaway and has become a favorite tourist attraction for those traveling by automobile or bicycle and even by walking.

After I left Japan and returned home I found myself in a quandary. What have I learned about Buddhism? This first trip left me more perplexed than before I started. I knew I would have to learn more and seek guidance. Like so many who chose to explore Buddhism as part of an alternative lifestyle, my head was full of preconceived ideas about what Buddhism should be. I had read a little of what was available on Buddhism at the time, but knew nothing about Buddhism as it was actually practiced in Japan. One day I received an announcement from the Barre Center for Buddhist Studies in Barre, MA and decided to take a course in practicing meditation with the resident teacher at the time, Mu Soeng Sunim, a Korean Kwan Um monk. Actually he is an Indian but he studied and was ordained in the Kwan Um tradition at a Korean monastery in Cumberland, RI. The course was easy to follow and I learned the practice particulars quickly. I had an opportunity to read and study Dogen's Manual of

Zen Meditation by Carl Bielefeldt which gave me a much better insight into the Zen practice. Some time later I returned to the Barre Center with my friend Maury (Dr. Maurice Siegel) only to find that Mu Soeng had disrobed voluntarily. He told me that since becoming the director of the Barre Center, a promotion, he decided to disrobe after eleven years as a practicing monk. He looked very different wearing civilian mufti and allowing his hair to grow out. Whatever the reason I found him to be a worthy teacher and Buddhist scholar. We became fast friends and I attended several classes which he taught on different Buddhist subjects, particularly the Heart Sutra and the Diamond Sutra.

One day at lunch we discussed our individual upbringing. I was surprised to learn that we shared similar backgrounds. We both began in our youth as devotees of Marxism. In Marxism I found for the first time a combination of the language of science and the language of myth – a union of mysticism and logic. Scientific agnosticism was an austere self-denial in a world inherently lifeless and undramatic, a world with neither purpose nor climax. Social movements had assumed the character of a superficial altruistic anodyne ungrounded in the nature of the universe. In Marxism, however, one's ideals could be taken as expressions of an underlying historical necessity in things.

In adolescence I was to discover the new philosophy of Existentialism. In particular I. admired the writings of Albert Camus. Whereas Marxism speaks to the exploitation of man, Existentialism describes man's anguish and despair. The Existentialist shares with the Marxist a feeling of responsibility for the condition of man, a conception of life as perpetual warfare, and a willingness to engage his weapons as a thinker in battle. The most urgent battles are those which are fought out on the political battlefield.

Now, in my senior years, I am asking the question – Can it be that man's life was meant to be unsatisfactory? In Buddhism this question is answered through an understanding of the causal law. According to Buddha's teaching there is nothing in this world that does not come within the realm of the causal law. Causality explains the arising and passing away of things. Hence, the direct corollaries of the theory of causality are that all things in this world are (1) impermanent (*anicca*), (2) unsatisfactory (*dukkha*), and (3) non-substantial (*anatman*). From the fact of the impermanence of the world, it follows that all things are unsatisfactory (*dukkha*). Early Buddhism never denied the satisfaction that man can derive from worldly things. While not denying satisfaction, it emphasizes the fact that this satisfaction is generally followed by evil or harmful consequences. This is true for several reasons. The nature of man is such that he craves for eternal or permanent happiness. But the things from which he hopes to derive such happiness are themselves impermanent. Happiness or satisfaction derived from impermanent or ephemeral things would surely be temporary and therefore fall short of his expectation, that is, permanent happiness - hence his suffering. The things from which he tries to drive satisfaction may, therefore, in the ultimate analysis, be unsatisfactory. Thus, it seems that human suffering is due to attachment to the things that are themselves unsatisfactory.

Ever since completing the first trip I prepared myself both intellectually and pragmatically for the time when I would return to Japan to continue seeking the Buddhist ethic. The next thing I did was to return to the Barre Center for Buddhist Studies in order to engage under the tutelage of Dr. Andrew Olendzki in order to receive basic Buddhist information. He was giving a three-part course as follows:

The life of Buddha – (The Historical Buddha) – October 3

The World of Buddha – (Life and Society in Ancient India) – November 7

The Birth of Buddha – (Early Buddhism as a Social and Religious Movement) – December 12

As it turned out this was necessary and important information for an objective understanding before attempting the second trip which would involve a pilgrimage with a practice of Buddhism in an esoteric milieu.

During the ten years between the two trips I had practiced zazen (Zen meditation) at the Minnesota Zen Meditation Center in Minneapolis, MN, the Mt. Tremper Monastery in Mt. Tremper, NY, the Rochester Zen Center in Rochester, NY, the Dai Bosatsu Monastery in Livingston Manor, NY, the Chuang Yen Monastery in Carmel, NY, and the Shobo-Ji Temple in New York City, NY. I now felt amply prepared and ready to travel back to Japan and continue my search for the Buddha.

Seto Naikai The Inland Sea

Canal In Kurashiki

Itskushima

Archeology Museum Kurashiki

Korakuen Gardens Okayama

THE SECOND TRIP

THE DIVINE WALK

A JOURNEY IN SEARCH OF THE BUDDHIST ETHIC

I – HOMAGE TO KUKAI

I was getting slightly dizzy as the cable car climbed the mountain. It was a cool and salubrious day and the light of the sun was blocked by the forest of trees on both sides of the cable car pathway making it appear to be going through a tunnel. It produced a gentle vertigo, a vague numbness, which submerged the memory of everything bad – pain and confusion, desire and ambition – in lethargic bliss. As we reached the top there was a break in the wall of trees and once again we arrived in the bright sunshine. The cable car began to empty out of its anxious tourists who came to Mount Koya to visit the various temple sites and enjoy a day of frolic.

Following the crowd to the bus station I found that people were jabbering incessantly and although the utterances were incoherent to me they obviously understood each other with broad smiles and occasional laughter. I then came upon hundreds of screaming schoolchildren, all girls. Apparently it was a holiday called National Children's Day for girls. It seemed every schoolgirl in Japan was going to Mt. Koya. They did what schoolgirls everywhere do. They laughed, they shrieked, they burst into hysterical sobs – all for no apparent reason. Some people bought articles at the stalls, which lined the front of the station. After taking the bus for the short ride to the temple and cemetery, I strode through the long entrance hall and across that delightful garden, where the gravel of its pathway would grate beneath my feet.

There among the trees is the ancient stone tomb of Kukai, better known by his posthumous title, Kobo Daishi. I looked down the mile-long path that disappears under the cedars, as the tops of the cedars themselves disappear in the mist. Mt. Koya is the headquarters of the Shingon sect. It is a holy site to practice Tantric Buddhism in the presence of Kobo Daishi, who resides there in eternal meditation. Incorporating a bizarre, exhilarating mixture of the sacred and the profane, the sublime and the hideous, transcendental wisdom and crude superstition, the charm of Mt. Koya is impossible to describe.

Shivering, even though the weather is slightly warm, I bow before the gravesite and ask that the Daishi be with me on my pilgrimage. There were many tombstones mossy with age, clean fragrant air, and a sense of great peace. I walked back through the darkening shade toward the temple Shinnoin where I am to lodge. This temple among the many that are here on this Buddhist Mountain is filled with worshipers. They light their candles and their sticks of incense, adding them to banks of flame and urns that issue clouds of scented smoke. The Head Priest Zenkyo Nakagawa beseeches the Daishi's intercession for a petitioner who stands beside him. Presently they move together to stand before the tomb.

In 774 the future Kukai was born to Lady Tamayori and Saeki Tagimi, members of a declining aristocracy, in the province of Sanuki on the island of Shikoku. While in college Kukai became dissatisfied with his Confucian studies and so turned to Buddhism in search for higher spiritual values. At twenty, led by the Abbot of Yuwabuchi, he went to the Makinosan Temple, and there he shaved his head and received the Ten Precepts.

In the latter half of the eighth century certain Nara monks, dissatisfied with the vain, pompous affairs of the urban Buddhist establishments, built temples in secluded mountains for the practice of meditation. At the start of his spiritual quest, Kukai most likely joined this group as a private priest. His interest in Buddhism arose not so much from book learning as from actual experience of meditation. When traveling and begging for food as a wandering ascetic, Kukai came face to face with native ways of life and with gods, or kami. He felt a close affinity between nature and man. Such predilections prompted him to build his monastic center on remote Mt. Koya. Kukai alternated between Mt. Koya and Kyoto.

While in Kyoto at the Takaosanji, Kukai began to establish himself as the religious and cultural leader of early Heian society (794-1185).

Emperor Saga was the promoter of Kukai. He appointed Kukai as administrative head *(betto)* of the Todaiji in Nara and granted Kukai permission to perform an esoteric Buddhist ceremony at the Takaosanji. Kukai's later success in superimposing his own esotericism, known as Shingon, on Nara Buddhism started with his appointment from 810 to 813. In 816 he was granted permission to build a monastic center on Mt. Koya. In 835 he passed away on Mt. Koya.

The Holy Men, resplendent evangelists of medieval times, transformed Kukai into a saint and a savior. They created a deity, and their faith gave rise to the pilgrimage, which encircles Kukai's home island. Pilgrims walk the course today as they have for centuries convinced that Kukai is walking with them. These pilgrims are known as Henro pilgrims, committed to the eighty- eight sacred places of Shikoku.

I left Mt. Koya the next day by going down with the cable car and thence taking the train back to Kyoto where I was staying at the Ryokan Hiraiwa. I had planned on making the pilgrimage the next day by taking the train to Kobe and thence by boat to Takamatsu and starting at Temple 68, Jinne-in. Most people, however, leave Mt. Koya and go across the wide strait by ferry to Shikoku to Temple number one, Ryozenji in Tokushima. This pilgrimage is essentially a circle. A circle has no beginning and no end and so it can be properly started at any point. This pilgrimage has no goal, in the usual sense, except to close the circle by returning to one's starting point.

While I was in Kyoto I spent several days visiting the Higashi Hongwanji Temple, which celebrates Shinran as an *arhat* (saint). It was there I met Hiroshi Hideki, a gruff fellow with a freckled pate. He had the most homely features imaginable: a full moon of a face, pitted with little holes and disfigured with pimples, a bottle nose, a nebulous chin, reddish cheeks covered with strong stubble of beard, a short bull neck. He was a good-natured, roistering sort of fellow. He appeared too embonpoint for a Japanese man. He spoke fairly good English with cackling jocosity. He was wearing neither kingly robes nor peasant garb. But he did spend much time with me explaining the history of Kobo Daishi and the selection of Mt. Koya as the training center for Shingon Buddhism.

Hundreds of works of religious art were collected and preserved at Mt. Koya including treasures of Shingon Mikkyo (mystical or Tantric Buddhism) itself and other forms of Buddhism, of Shinto, Shugen, and syncretic practice – each an expression of faith and many influential in the development of Japanese religious thought and culture.

Hiroshi told me that when I visit the Shikoku 88 Reijo (holy places), I would receive a *Fuda* as a record of my pilgrimage at the first temple I visit. This Fuda is stamped with the temple seal at each subsequent temple I visit until the entire map is complete. This is said to have been established by Kobo Daishi himself in the 9th century. But it is interesting that a similar practice is performed at the Santiago Campostela pilgrimage in Spain. Visiting the 88 Reijo is a form of faith in Kobo Daishi. People go on a pilgrimage totaling 1450 km. (878 miles) to all 88 Reijo to have their prayers answered. On foot, it takes 40 to 60 days to visit all 88 Reijo. The paths to the Reijo are full of high and steep mountains and ocean cliffs, and are said to be the roughest paths of all, now as well as in olden days.

Hiroshi wished me luck in my quest and gave me a walking stick as a parting gift. It was made of bamboo with a copper tip and a brass top: obviously, homemade. He said that the staff represents Kobo Daishi as it travels with every pilgrim. The staff is a pilgrim's most important possession, and its tip and base – its face and feet – should be washed carefully at every overnight stop, even before one washes oneself. I was touched by this gesture and promised to write him when I completed my tour of the 88 Reijo. He gave me his address and we parted with low bows. I felt excited and yet apprehensive at the prospect of my new adventure. Returning to my ryokan I packed my gear and prepared myself for the boat ride tomorrow to the city of Takamatsu where I expect eventually to take a train to Temple 68, Jinne-in.

II - TAKAMATSU

All the way to the horizon in the last light, the sea was just degrees of gray, rolling and frothy on the surface. The waves looked like hills coming up from behind, and most of the crew seemed not to glance at them. There were no other boats in sight, but off to the rear for a while one could see the reassuring outlines of the coast of Honshu. Then it got dark. The boat rocked one way, gave a loud thump, and then it rolled the other. The pots and pans in the galley clanged. A chair which someone had forgotten to stow away, slid back and forth across the cabin floor, over and over again. Sometime late that night, one of the crew raised a voice against the wind and shouted, "Joriku, joriku" (landing soon).

Most of the crew now fell into that half-autistic state that the monotony of storms at sea occasionally induces. You find a place to sit and getting a good hold of it, you try not to move again. The boat rolls this way and you flex the muscles around your stomach, and then relax, she rolls that way and you flex again.

When we "set sail" from Toshin Pier in sheltered Kobe harbor earlier in the evening, I felt at least a little bit romantic. But when we cleared the lee of the land and entered the seaway, and the boat began to lurch, I grabbed the nearest sturdy thing as I veered and tacked across the tilting floor. By the time it got dark, I almost lost my supper. It was the beginning of a storm at sea. I had engaged this small boat with other people, mostly working class, because it was the cheapest way to get to Shikoku. The other passengers brought their goods on board in bundles, boxes, baskets, wicker crates and cardboard suitcases and headed down steep iron stairs for the communal sitting/sleeping room below. I elected to remain on deck in order to avoid the nauseating odors downstairs.

As we neared shore the storm seemed to gain in intensity. I dis-embarked and headed for shore with a line of passengers going down the gangplank, all hurrying to avoid getting caught in the storm. I headed with my shoulder pack for the Ryokan Shintokiwa about a fifteen-minute walk from the pier on Mizuki-dori Street. It was a small ryokan which comprises a two-storey building giving directly on to the street, and a large hall with windows, set among arbores-cent lilac trees that are fragrant from April onwards.

It has been many years since my last visit to the Marine City of Takamatsu. I remember Takamatsu City as an outstanding example of a sightseeing spot in Shikoku, rich in notable places and historical relics such as Ritsurin Park and Takamatsu Joshi (Takamatsu Castle Ruins).

In the center of the city, fashionable shopping arcades intersect or run parallel on a scale that is nearly unparalleled in western Ja-pan. I remember, quite fondly, various attractions, which are scat-tered around the surrounding area, such as Chuo Koen (Central Park), which seemed like an oasis of green trees, the Takamatsu Art Museum, which boasts a collection of masterpieces by such re-nowned artists as Picasso and Matisse, or the Kagawaken Kemmin Hall (Kagawa Prefectural Citizens Hall), with the latest theatrical facilities.

For a supposed backwater Takamatsu is, in some ways, more sophisticated than Tokyo or Osaka. Of course, while here, I intend visiting them all. I will first focus on Takamatsu Joshi (Takamatsu Castle Ruins), which is located just east of the JR Station. There I shall be able to get information and a timetable of trains on the Yo-san line to Temple 68. The castle was built facing the Seto Inland Sea and is surrounded on its three other sides with moats fed by the sea. It is truly a wonder to behold.

As I hurried along I could not help but noticing the many gar-dens that I passed.

The secret in a Japanese garden is that they do not attempt too much. That reserve and sense of propriety, which characterize this people in all their decorative and other artistic work are here seen to perfection. Furthermore, in the midst of so much that is evanescent they see the necessity of providing enduring points of interest in the way of little ponds and bridges, odd-shaped stone lanterns and inscribed rocks and rustic fences, quaint paths of stone and pebble, and always a number of evergreen trees and shrubs.

The Japanese have brought their garden arts to such perfection that a plot of ground ten feet square is capable of being exquisitely beautified by their methods.With cleanliness, simplicity, a few little evergreen shrubs, one or two little clusters of flowers, a rustic fence projecting from the side of the house, a quaintly shaped flower- pot or two, containing a few choice plants, - the simplest form of garden is attained.

So much do the Japanese admire gardens, and garden effects, that their smallest strips of ground are utilized for this purpose. In the crowded city, among the poorest houses, one often sees, in the corner of a little earth-area that comes between the sill and the raised floor, a miniature garden made in some shallow box, or even on the ground itself.

Thus I saw these delightful little gardens as I hurried along. The weather was becoming evermore threatening. My legs were aching as I ran in short bursts. My heart was pounding and my lungs were retching as I hurried along. A dryness appeared in my mouth caused by the continuous labored breathing with my mouth open. This was enough to permit a momentary stop. I threw my head back and breathed deeply as I relieved my shoulder ache by placing the bag on the ground. The wind seemed to be picking up while I repetitively inhaled and exhaled. I seemed to revive somewhat after this respite so I lifted the bag onto my shoulder once again and continued my journey.

I was then breathing naturally and freely as I walked along. A film of moisture began to condense upon my cold lips but my tongue enjoyed the feeling as it wiped the fleshy folds a trifle. An expiration of air caused a single painful utterance, "Oh! Oh!" I was aware that I had to reach the ryokan soon or collapse from exhaustion.

The sky darkened as the scudding clouds blanketed the area and the wind gusted in ever greater intensity. These changes gave me the impetus to quicken my gait. I began to falter as I trotted along with an increasing stride at a breakneck jogging pace. My shoulder bag kept bouncing on my rump in rhythm with my running. At any moment I expected the heavens to open up and shower the earth copiously. In reality a watery mist was beginning to form in the atmosphere which gave me pause. As tired as I was I decided to not yield to fatigue until I reached the ryokan.

At last I could see the ryokan in the distance. It seemed like an oasis for me to reach. I found my body sweating and my shoulder aching from carrying the shoulder-strap bag as I hurried along to reach the ryokan. I was very tired and exhausted from the enervating and debilitating boat trip. I almost tripped and fell as I tried walking faster. Yet, I noticed the dispersal of people to avoid the coming storm.

The storm which had long been perceptible to my senses was now unmistakably approaching. Great clouds seemed to clatter against one another like heavy blank chests above the tremulous, quivering treetops, which were lit now and then by pale darting tongues of lightening. There was an acrid smell in the damp air, which was tossed hither and thither by squally gusts. The town seemed quite changed; the streets were quite different, as I now hurried to the ryokan. A few minutes before they had lain with bated breath in the pale moonlight; now the street signs clanked and clattered as though startled out of an oppressive dream, doors rattled uneasily, chimney-pots groaned, in some houses inquisitive lights were turned on, and here and there white-clad figures could be seen cautiously shutting the windows against the approaching storm. The few belated passersby scurried from street-corner to street-corner as though driven along by the very breath of fear. I hoped to get to the ryokan before the storm broke.

Just as I arrived at the ryokan it started raining with fierce, biting pelts of raindrops. I registered at the front desk after removing my shoes at the threshold of the inn and donned the provided house slippers. I left the slippers outside my room and entered. The room is a single, large undivided room floored with traditional rice-straw tatami matting. It functions as a living room during the day and as a bedroom during the night with comfortable futon bedding being laid out. The bedding is stored in rolled up condition in the closet. After the tiresome voyage and the oppressive storm I felt I needed a relaxing bath. The bath and toilet facilities are separate from the room and are shared by staying guests. I undressed and put on the provided unlined cotton yukata, which serves as a bathrobe. Entering the bath requires changing the soft cotton house slippers for plastic slippers. I then proceeded to give my body a washing with a soapy cloth and a loofah. Upon completion I rinsed off the soapy lather with a bucket of clear water. I entered the tub and began immediately to soak and relax my tired muscles in the tepid water. The water was very warm and stimulating. After a short while I decided to leave the tub, followed by a rub down with a towel. I put on the yukata garment and headed for my room. Using the yukata as a pajama I crawled into my futon and fell fast asleep.

The next morning I awoke at 4:30 am and headed for the bathroom to shower, shave, and brush my teeth. Returning to my room, I sat in zazen meditation for the usual forty minutes. This ryokan provides two Japanese-style meals – breakfast and dinner. Breakfast begins at 6:00 am so I had less than an hour to plan the two days I expected to spend in Takamatsu. Breakfast consisted of a bowl of cooked rice (gohan) plus a piece of fish, sautéed in hot oil and soy sauce, and a bowl of miso soup and a pot of green tea. After finishing breakfast, I decided to walk towards the pier in order to view the Takamatsu Castle ruins (Takamatsu Joshi) just east of the JR Takamatsu station. The castle was built in 1590 facing the Seto Inland Sea (Seto Nagai) and is surrounded on its three other sides with moats fed by the sea. It is one of the "Three Seaside Castles of Japan". Today, the site of the ancient castle has been made into Tamamo Koen (Tamamo Park) which seemed like an oasis of green trees with a spreading parterre of brilliant green lawns edged by ancient oaks and elms and classic geometry of flower beds orchestrated by unseen master gardeners into a four-season symphony of color. I was particularly struck by the plethora of various colored azaleas, orange, white, red, and purple. Some of the local streets were boulevards with central dividers made of azalea hedging of various colors.

In the late afternoon, I walked towards the Takamatsu Art Museum. This brought me through a maze of winding streets forming little private villages, self-contained and quite mysterious. Each neighborhood has its own markets, little vegetable stores, fish stores, coffeehouses and restaurants. The homes are hidden behind walls covered with the over hanging branches of large trees. Once in a while, there will be a small niche in the wall, holding a Buddha with a bib around his neck and an altar with flowers.

I decide to have lunch in a small noodle restaurant called Namiki Yabusoba, run by a master chef. Here everything is made from noodles: fried noodles served with vinegar and honey sauce; noodles in soup with fried fish, shrimp or pork; tender sushi filled with noodles and fresh fish; cold noodles in a basket served with a light soy sauce and fresh grated wasabi (horseradish); noodles in a pot (a sort of soup with fish cake); fresh shiitaki mushrooms and sliced trefoil (an herb from the parsley family) ...the choices are unlimited, the noodles superb.

Well-fed and happy, I walked on to the Takamatsu Art Museum that boasts a collection of masterpieces by such artists as Picasso and Matisse as well as a large display of Asian art.

I was particularly interested in the Picasso paintings having visited Picasso museums in most parts of the world – Mexico City and Paris. This museum had a wonderful collection of Picasso prints as well as paintings. Picasso's production as a printmaker was enormous, with over 2000 prints catalogued in all. In this collection there were several, which were an effective means of political expression: to protest against Franco's coup d'etat in 1937. Picasso printed two plates to accompany one of his poems, Sugno y Mentira de Franco (Dream and Lie of Franco). He also made a print called, The Weeping Woman, whose tormented face denounces the horrors of war.

There were three paintings by Matisse in the collection; a portrait of Matisse's daughter, Marguerite, painted in 1907 and the masterful, Still Life with Oranges, undeniably the outstanding masterpiece of the collection. Finally, there is the Seated Young Girl of 1942. It is interesting to me that these two artists who were friends should be represented together in this museum. It is well known that they influenced each other in their choice of subject matter and their use of form and color. They were not competitors in the usual sense but they fed off of each other and were well aware of their greatness. When Matisse died Picasso was devastated. Picasso went on to live well into his 90's still very productive.

After two hours in the museum I walked back to my ryokan for a rest. In my room I found a freshly washed and ironed yukata and a tray with a hot water bottle (oyu) and a canister of green tea (ryokucha), perfect after a day of museuming and walking through the streets of Takamatsu. I rested and read for a while. After a while, the Okusan (mistress of the house) brought my dinner on a large tray. There was abalone with cucumber and sesame seeds in a bean curd sauce. This was followed by a bowl of wanmori: matsutake mushrooms served with warm nori with a thin slice of yuzu, a fragrant Japanese citrus fruit. Then Yakimono fish broiled to perfection together with egg plant and the ubiquitous cooked rice (gohan). The dinner was more than unforgettable.

Later that evening, I decide to go to Kagawaken Kemmin (Kagawaka Prefectural Citizen's Hall) to hear a performance of the Osaka Philharmonic Orchestra conducted by Koichiro Harada with piano soloist Harumi Hanafusa. The tickets were expensive but well worth it to hear such a talented and professional music group. When one thinks of Japanese music, the principal traditions of Buddhist chant come to mind. These chants have always been those of the Tendai and Shingon sects, both founded in the early 9th century. Later on the Edo period (1603-1867) is characterized by the emergence of solo and chamber music for koto, shakuhachi and shamisen. This traditional music is a far cry from the modern, European program I heard that night: Tchaikovsky's Fifth Symphony and the Tchaikovsky Piano Concerto. The pieces were played superbly with great verve and vigor. The hall had wonderful acoustics and the nearly sold out audience seemed entranced by the skill of the musicians.

The next day, after a breakfast of suppon (cold turtle soup) and congee (Sanskrit for rice porridge) flecked with ground sesame seeds and a side dish of pickled vegetables and the usual pot of green tea, I went to the Takamatsu JR Station to make train schedule inquiries. It is my intention to take the JR Yosan line tomorrow to Kan-Onji and start the pilgrimage at Temple 68, Jinne-in. I received a timetable from the stationmaster and discovered that the earliest train was 6:00 am. Armed with this information I decided to visit Ritsurin Park.

Ritsurin Park is one of the most typical Japanese gardens spread over an area of approximately 650 acres. The park actually consists of two gardens, namely, the Northern and Southern. It was originally built 340 years ago as a villa of the then ruling feudal family, the Matsudairas. This promenade type of garden is most exquisitely laid out, against the background of Mt. Shiun, with rocks, ponds, and trees, each boasting a quaint beauty of its own and has been said to be the best of its kind in Japan. As I walked along to the south garden and pond I passed the Byobu Matsu or screen of pine trees and then suddenly came upon the "Cliff of Red Rock" which is actually Red Waii trees. The Kikugetsu-tei (moon scooping summer house) viewed across the south pond was a startling sight. This house is the former tea ceremony house of the Matsudairas. In order to get there I had to walk across the half-moon bridge which spanned across the south pond. This was a most memorable event. In addition, I visited the Art Gallery, a folkcraft house and the Zoo.

I arrived back at the ryokan at about 5:00 pm in the afternoon, when the trees and shrubs had begun to cast long shadows over the garden's terracotta paths and the air at the ryokan was thick with the sound of crickets. I sought out the proprietor and spoke with him in my faulty Japanese, which was liberally sprinkled with Pidgin English. We managed somehow to understand each other. After a good many years of desultory travel in Japan I devised an adequate method of communication using some Japanese, some English and some hand gestures.

The proprietor of the ryokan whose name is Hirano Yuichi, looks as he should, high forehead, eagle nose, broad in the shoulders, narrow in the hip. Average height, brooding, dressed in a brown, two-piece plain cloth work suit. He had large eyes and long lashes like a girl's. His strides can seem too long for his legs, but he is a light-footed man, nevertheless.

I walked up to him with hands together and bowed.

"I shall be leaving tomorrow morning to start the *henro* pilgrimage", I said in a deep voice.

He looked at me querulously before commenting, "I see. What time will you leave?"

"I must catch the six o'clock train in the morning." I answered.

He hesitated for a moment then responded," If you like we can have some breakfast ready for you at five o'clock."

I was amazed at this courtesy but quickly answered, "Thank you. That would be very nice. As a favor, may I leave one bag until I return? It may be a month or so."

He quickly responded, "Of course, but please be sure there are no valuables."

I eagerly thanked him, "I would like to pay my bill now."

He went behind the counter and removed a sheet of paper from the drawer and handed it to me. After scrutinizing the bill I gave him my credit card.

Morning came, rapid and intolerant; the way morning is in the tropics. As usual it was the city that woke me with its shrugging, careless noise of shouts and engines and bicycle bells. Crows sat on the windowsills, bold as brass, and cawed me out of my futon. But in spite of all the noise, it was a silence that dragged me upright, a silence where there should have been sound. There were no household noises. But I could hear the Okusan shuffling outside my door. She brought me a bowl of thick rice *congee* (porridge) with a small piece of *butaniku* (pork) and a pot of green tea. I thanked her profusely and commenced eating. Having completed my meal and my toilet, I said goodbye and proceeded on my way to the JR station carrying only my walking stick, a small shoulder bag and wearing a white *chapeau bras,* which can be folded and placed in my pocket. The sun rose, unwrapping the misty city like a gift.

III – JINNE-IN

I embarked on the train of the Yosan line heading for the town of Kan-Oji and Temple 68, Jinne-in. According to my map there is a cluster of three temples in that area, Temple 69, Kan-oji and Temple 70, Motoyamaji, as well as Temple 68, Jinne-in.

The train followed the shore route, which was very beautiful. Heading west along the *Seto Nagai* (inland sea) the view across the water sparkled with the rising sun like camera flashes seen in a dark auditorium. Viewed from the scenic skyline route above the sea below, the panoramic vistas are truly breathtaking. Countless small inlets dot the horizon creating a calm, but exotic atmosphere. Blessed with one of the most spectacular coastlines in all of Japan, the azure waters of Kanagawa prefecture provide both vitality to the local economy and many recreational opportunities to residents. Moving south, the coast gradually becomes more spectacular as the deep blue color of the sea is enhanced by lush green vegetation and crisp, white waves.

At last after a two-hour train ride, we arrived at Kan-Oji station. I disembarked with a mixed group of people. Some wore the distinctive uniform of the *henro* pilgrimage – white pants and white shirt, head covered with a conical fiber hat, leggings and imitation straw sandals and a walking stick called a *kongozue*. Several had a black neck ribbon inscribed with Japanese characters. A local temple to represent them on the pilgrimage could have provided this.The one I wore represented the Higashi Hongwanji Temple in Kyoto and was a deep, brilliant mauve color with gold characters.

A group of us walked along a dirt road following a map that pointed the way. Onlookers along the roadside waved at us and hurled expressions of encouragement. Occasionally, an automobile would drive by with the driver waving his right arm. Traffic in Japan is on the left side – driver on the right side as in England. I have since learned that many people do the pilgrimage by automobile instead of walking.

After a short while we came upon a long thicket of red bougainvillea mixed in with white columbine, which acted like a living fence. Just ahead on a winding path was the temple, number 68, Jinne-in. I approached the entrance with trepidation. After all I was the only westerner and a stranger to the culture.

The temple supervisor, dressed in black robes, clutched his hands in Oriental supplication and greeted the entering throng of pilgrims with nods, bows and a broad grin. An electric fan whined uselessly in one corner next to an ancient statue of the *Kannon* (goddess of compassion). The air inside the temple stank of a mustiness probably caused by the burning incense and body odor of the pilgrims milling about. The temple supervisor was a dark complected man in his early thirties of stately frame, whose round somewhat bloated face is without a trace of beard. It wasn't just clean-shaven; one would have been able to see some stubble. On the contrary, it was soft, bleary and boyish, nourishing only the occasional patch of down. And that looked very odd. The expression in his glassy, doe-brown eyes was mild, his nose squat and a bit too fleshy. What's more he had an arched Roman-looking upper lip and feet of unusual dimensions. He was unsociable, sharing nothing of himself with a single soul. Only occasionally a congenial, affable, even exuberant mood could steal over him.

He glanced briefly over at me with that attitude of absolute indifference, which almost has the appearance of contempt. I thought of something I could say, but didn't have the courage to say it. Here too it was the same as ever: they wouldn't understand me; they would only listen to what I had to say in embarrassing silence. For their language was not mine. Still, I ventured forth and decided to approach him

I blurted out, "Good morning, Reverend."

He snorted through one nostril to clear the passages and to my utter surprise spoke in perfect English.

"Good morning, sir."

I was momentarily discomfited by his attitude and speech.

I spoke rather quickly, "I would like to obtain a *Fuda*. I am making the complete *henro* pilgrimage but I am starting from here."

He answered gruffly, "We do not have any *Fudas* but they are available for about 100 yen at Temple number 1, Ryozen-ji in Tokushima. However, I can give you our temple seal on a piece of paper."

I thanked him respectfully, "Thank you. That would be satisfactory."

I followed him to a desk where he stamped a small piece of paper with the temple seal and gave it to me in cupped hands with a bow. I then went to the shrine and lit three pieces of incense, bowed three times before the statue of Buddha and placed the incense in a censor on a table, which also had a bowl of fruit. I then turned around and noticed the other people. One could distinguish the native from the *peregrini*, the foreigners and pilgrims who come to Shikoku for the *henro*. I felt I was something of a religious tourist, floundering about in search of a spiritual path that would suit my own moral and personal inclinations.

A man's life, Kukai taught his monks, did not move in a linear progression, with each day an equal chit on the calendar of existence. Rather it moved from defining moment to defining moment, marked by the decisions that roiled the soul. Here was such a moment, I thought. I could start here and now or I could turn around being true to all that passed as virtue in the world.

I placed several coins in the donation box and walked outside to look at the structure of the temple. It was an old wooden building with a thatched roof and outside plastered walls some of whose parts were in a dilapidated condition with bamboo slats exposed. It actually looked more like a dwelling than a temple. The gable ends showing, in their exterior, massive timbers roughly hewn, with all the irregularities of the tree-trunk preserved.

I walked on down the path, following two women who were chattering and talking unintelligibly; at least to me it seemed like incoherent utterances. Finally, I reached the dirt road and looked over the expanse of heather and small hills rolling like a sea toward the horizon. Sparrows flitter among the heather. The white pines were a wall of green, a blur of jade where the blue sky had been. I kept on walking, more like trudging, which lifted small clouds of dust beneath my feet.

One comes upon Temple 69, Kannon-ji abruptly, as if a curtain had been pulled back on the arid mountainous pines, lowland desert growth, and thorny mesquite that make up the characteristic face of the mountains in Kanagawa Prefecture in the northwestern Shikoku. A trail along the edge of the dry upland pines follows a short decline around a mountain bend and opens up to reveal the Temple 69, Kannon-ji with its broadleaf deciduous trees surrounding the building. One instantly notices big butterflies, soaring in groups of ten or more over the ravines, back and forth from the high trees on one side to those on the other. When I approached the temple building, I noticed no one about. For a long time, during my trek, I noticed none of the pilgrims from Temple 68; Jinne-in took the same route as me. I did not think much about this at the time but now I wondered what was wrong. There was a small shed at the side of the temple building in which an old man resided. He was of average height, broad-shouldered, strong and short-legged, possessing a full red face, aquamarine eyes shadowed by very light gray brows, wide nostrils and moist lips.

I approached saying, "Good morning, Venerable Master. Is the temple closed?"

He smiled while remarking, "Yes, it is closed. There is no priest. I am the caretaker not a master."

I questioned with a frown, "Why is it closed? I was given to understand that all the 88 Reijo temples of the pilgrimage were open."

He seemed very chary of revealing its secrets but continued in a slow, methodical, accretive voice.

He seemed to delight in revealing some information, " Kannon-ji and Jinne-in now occupy the same compound; they constitute one temple but two Sacred Places. Even though they are both of the Shingon sect the deity of Jinne-in is Amida Buddha while the deity of Kannon-ji is Kannon."

I flustered, "I see. Then all the other temples of the pilgrimage are open."

He answered forthrightly, "Yes. Would you like to join me in some tea while you rest from your journey?"

I was amazed at his kindness but quickly accepted with a bow, "Thank you very much."

We then both sat at the table while he poured the tea.

He looked at me with watery eyes as he said, "My name is Kuruma Jinan."

I bowed and responded with a slight grin, "My name is Shansky Albert."

Japanese nomenclature is hierarchical – the first of the two names is actually a category and is able to contain one or more members going by a second name, just like the surname of a family in English and is roughly equivalent to the "last name first, first name last" convention.

As we sat drinking the hot, green liquid, a conversation arose

He politely questioned, "Is this your first visit to Shikoku, Shansky-kun?"(Mr. Shansky)

I answered, "No. I first came here in 1975 to visit Yashima in Takamatsu. At that time there were no bridges connecting Shikoku Island to the Honshu mainland. Now there are three bridges, the Kuroshima-Kaikyo Bridge, the Seto-Ohashi Bridge over which the

JR Railway travels, and the Onaruto Bridge. In 1975 I had to come by boat from Uno as I did this time from Kobe.

He looked at me strangely before asking, "What did you do at Yashima?"

I became quite pedantic in my answer, "Yashima is about 3 and ¾ miles east of Takamatsu. It is a small hill made up of lava and extends like a ridge of a mountain. It was once an island, but it is now connected with the mainland of Shikoku by a narrow strip of land.

He looked at me questioningly, "I am curious what you did there, Shansky-kun." (Mr. Shansky)

I continued with my elaborate answer, "Yashima is famed for its magnificent views and as the refuge of the Taira Clan. It is the scene of a major encounter between two clans some 800 years ago. I have a book at home describing the battle. After reading it I vowed one day to visit Yashima. By the way, on the top of the south ridge, which commands an impressive view of the Inland Sea, stands Yashima-ji temple, which contains many relics from battles between the two rival clans."

He looked at me with a glassy stare, "I never knew a *Gaijin* (foreigner) who knew so much about Japanese history. What was your reason for going on the Henro pilgrimage?"

I answered, "I am interested in Buddhism and I thought I might become aware of the Buddha's teachings and ethics if I made this trip. The Buddha, Siddharta Gautama, lived and taught over 2500 years ago. His teachings comprised some of the highest moral philosophy then known to man and appealed to the rational and poetic minds alike. He led a remarkable life, traveling and teaching ceaselessly for forty-five years after attaining enlightenment. I am attempting to bring Buddha alive through this pilgrimage by interweaving actual events from his life with fictional encounters."

He responded, "This custom of making pilgrimages has been popular since the beginning of the Edo Period (1603-1867), and nowadays the number of pilgrims who complete their visit to the 88 temples by bus in 13 days amounts to about 100,000 annually. The way you are going, on foot, will take more than a month."

I stated, "I knew some people went by automobile but I never realized that tour companies were providing bus tours."

He laughed, "Yes. They come but with very little interest in the reason why Kukai established these temples. To most tourists it is just an accomplishment to make the trip and look at the beautiful scenery."

I questioned, "Well, Kuruma-san isn't there any Buddhist obeisance involved in their trip around the island?"

> He said with a deep voice, "Buddhist morality is not a matter of obeying a list of moral imperatives, motivated by fear. It's rather a matter of cultivating awareness of the effect of one's actions with positive and negative karmic results, and acting accordingly."

I was stymied, "I see. Thank you for your advice and hospitality. Now, I must be on my way to Temple 70, Motoyama-ji."

I bowed low and left the shed. I turned half way down the path to wave but the caretaker was nowhere to be seen. I made my way back to the same road to retrace my steps. I hastily decided to side trip and visit Kotobiki Park, where amidst hundreds of fantastic pines with gnarled and twisted roots, is a beach with what are called *zenigata*. These are a series of ditches dug in a form resembling an old coin. They are devised to look like a slotted coin many times magnified. I really enjoyed seeing these natural phenomena but felt the urgency and immediacy to continue my journey.

After an hour of walking I came to a little roadside fruit shop (*kudamonoya*). I stopped in and bought two Fuji apples for lunch. Fuji apples are immense and they are very crisp and meaty. After finishing my meager meal in the early afternoon, I began the journey out of the ravine, a steep uphill walk much more demanding than the morning trek in, and all the more exhausting because of the torrid sun. At one spot along the high ridge, an immense blackbird rookery set up a constant din, which could be heard from hundreds of yards away.

Paradoxically, this bedlam, a mix of thousands of frantic screeches and the churn of wind in the surrounding pines, never failed to induce in me, as I rested from my climb, a sense of perfect tranquility. It was a feeling of being utterly alone yet somehow comforted by the bird's chatter, as if on another plane of natural consciousness.

It is raining now, a fine icy drizzle that inserts itself between my clothes and me. I began walking again. When I came to a glade with a spring welling out of the base of a mossy rock, I knelt to drink the water from my hands and felt the peace and beauty of the valley flow into my body. I sensed something of it would be carried back to my life at home. In coming to this place, I had touched a hidden source within myself. After slaking the thirst produced by the apples I ate for lunch, I continued walking, as the rain stopped, until I reached the main road. After crossing over the main road, being careful to avoid traffic, I came upon a smaller road upon which I found several pilgrims walking. We greeted each other with shouts and joyous waving of arms. Suddenly, beyond the trees I spotted the temple. As I approached it I noticed the architecture was quite different than temple 68. For one thing, it had a tile roof. There is something truly majestic in the appearance of the broad and massive temple with grand upward sweep of the heavily tiled roof and deep shaded eaves, with an intricate maze of supports and carvings beneath; the whole sustained on colossal round posts locked and tied together by equally massive timbers. The effect is inspiring beyond description; and the contrast between this structure and the tiny and perishable dwellings that surround it render the former all the more grand and impressive.

IV – MOTOYAMA-JI

I was standing beside Temple 70, Motoyama-ji, which is located on a ridge, gazing out over the blue-green valleys of Shikoku set deep in ranges of shining peaks far off below me, where morning shadows still lingered, wisps of smoke from cooking fires floated like river mist over the small villages scattered between rice fields and forests of pine and rhododendrons. I entered the temple and found a large group of people milling about. I saw what I thought was the temple supervisor. He was a large jelly of a man, dressed in black robes, his head a hairless sun, a fiftyish fellow whom a lifetime of catering to pilgrims had failed to sour. But in spite of his habitual *bon homie* his expression darkened when I approached him.

I bowed and said, "Good day, honorable master."

He returned the bow and said, "Good day to you sir."

I asked, "Is it possible for me to purchase a Fuda at this temple?"

He looked at me with a smile, "Indeed, I have one right over here."

I was stunned for the moment having been told that I would have to wait until Temple number one to purchase a Fuda. I followed him eagerly to a desk underneath of which he removed a large sheet marked with the geographic outline of Shikoku.

He puffed as he straightened up, "Here it is; would you like me to write your name on it in Japanese?"

I quickly responded, "Oh yes, that would be very nice. My name is Shansky Albert."

He looked at me with his perpetual smile, "Well, since your name is a foreign one. I shall use *kana,* which are symbols. Each symbol represents the sound of one syllable. Your name Shansky would be Si ya n suki i."

He laughed as he printed the strokes of my name with a black brush pen.

He bellowed, "If you say it fast *san suki* in *kanji* (Japanese characters) would mean *thrice pleasing.*"

I laughed at his bit of jocosity.

I said, "I am very grateful for all your help but how do I handle the seal of Temple 68/69, which I have on this piece of paper?"

With a matter-of-fact movement he said, "We shall cut it out and paste it on the proper spot on the Fuda.

He proceeded to cut the seal with a scissor and pasted it on the designated mark on the Fuda. Then he stamped the Fuda with the seal of Temple 70. I thanked him profusely with many repetitive bows.

He immediately said, "The price of the Fuda is 100 yen."

I rummaged in my pocket, "Of course. Here is a 100-yen coin."

He took the coin and departed to join the other pilgrims. As my eyes followed him I saw a light on him, radiance, an aura, not excessive, but definitely emanating. We, the pilgrims, are shadowy bodies revolving around his sun. I walked over to the shrine and took three pieces of incense, lit them, and bowed three times before the Buddha. There was a large statue of Kannon slightly to the right of the Buddha. I bowed before her as well and then placed the incense in the censor on the table. Once again, I noticed a bowl of fruit on the table, but this time it was accompanied by several loose cigarettes. This seemed like a strange offering to me.

I left the temple, after placing some coins in the donation box, followed by a man in his late forties. He spoke in an exceedingly slow voice, almost robot-like.

He startled me as he spoke, "M-M-May I walk with you for a little while?"

I looked at him in assent. He was astonishingly small, very heavily bespectacled and bald. He had a terrible stammer when he spoke.

"I-I-I'm on my way to the t-t-train station. I am ending my p-p-pilgrimage here for now but I shall continue next year. I have been doing the Henro in segments for two years."

As I said, he was fortyish, small, and dark goateed and his sunglasses were made to fit his head, so that you never could catch a glimpse of his eyes, no matter how much you craned your curious neck. He spoke through teeth glittering in the most courteous of smiles.

He looked at me questioningly as he spoke in his stammering way, "I am c-c-curious, dear sir; do you think there is a G-G-God?"

I hesitated before answering, "Do you want my opinion?"

He seemed serious as he responded, "I would be m-m-most interested in your opinion, and forgive me for p-p prying."

This is a problem that has plagued me all my life. That is, the problem of God. Does God exist? I cannot call myself an atheist or an agnostic so often used by the laity. I prefer to call myself a nondeist, which still permits me belief in something. So I responded in the best way I knew how as we walked.

"There is no God except a man purified. And there is no Power exterior to him. There is no heaven or hell, good or evil, except that which he creates himself, and hence man is solely responsible to himself and to no one else."

He looked at me with serious eyes as he slowly responded, "Well, the more likely place to find G-G-God is along the margins of the world where people are starving, thirsty, homeless, imprisoned, bereaved, exiled, enslaved, oppressed, forgotten and dying. In these places are God's presence and God's ability to change the world."

I absorbed his statement for a while before answering, "I understand that our calling in life, like the calling of a musician or rather a blues guitarist is to create beauty out of joy and suffering. For me,

103

this calling is not fulfilled alone, but is instead collaborative. We compose our lives in collaboration with others and with the whole of creation. How alive Buddhism could become if we took its insights seriously. My reflections borrowed freely from process and traditional insights as well as from diverse literary sources focuses on grace-full, earthy, particular and sacramental moments to disclose the numinous. If there were a God what would be the value of faith? The fact that people have faith belies the existence of God."

He looked at me with a slight frown on his face, "It was very enlightening speaking with you, b-b-but I must leave you soon to get to the t-t-train station."

On the way back we fell in with a group of indigent farmers on their way to work in the rice paddies. I bade my companion a hearty goodbye and proceeded to walk across one of the rice paddies along the dike, which retains the flooded water. On the other side of the paddy I picked up the road once more and proceeded north, almost along the shoreline, to Temple 71, Iyadan-ji. As I strolled along, viewing the sea occasionally, I found my thoughts going to home. Will my wife and family believe this journey? My intellectual friends at home will think of me as an odd fish when I tell them about the places that I visited on this island. I can just hear them, "Don't you have anything better to do than torture yourself with bad hotels, and sleeping next to a fire on the cold ground?" How can I explain to them my quest for knowledge by living an ascetic existence? I can hardly explain it to myself; yet I am sure it is the right way.

*Every peasant shack I pass during my journey has
four or five friendly young faces looking out to greet
me. They are the future of this country.*

The buildings, on the cliffs about fifty feet above the sea, form a shelter from the strong winds that blow from landward in the late afternoons. Butterflies frequent the blooming legumes that dot the sandy open areas here, which, as one could tell by the deep black scars on many trees, had been burned over years before by a terrible fire. Dense clouds were rising above the mountains. There is nothing more frustrating than being caught in a sudden downpour. The clouds were boiling up and burning off magnificently. Amid a confusion of gray and white, the sun was working furiously to resurrect the day. Then, as is said by the Lithuanians, the day became as calm as a Belgian (Ref.: The Belgian Horse). In a little while I could see the temple almost hidden by the tall pines. I hurried along until I reached the gravel pathway. The loose rounded fragments made a solemn sound under my feet. There was a brush stand at the temple door to wipe my shoes before I entered the doorway. I removed my shoes after I entered. I noticed the large crowd in the main hall known as the *hatto*.

V – IYADAN-JI

I immediately spotted the temple supervisor. As usual, he wore black robes and carried himself with a certain amount of hauteur. He became the cynosure of critical eyes wearing thick, black rimmed glasses, cadaverous teeth, hairless head, ruthless, charming, insincere, every inch the embryonic cretin with an enigmatic little smile which I found almost insufferably pious. I walked over to the small group surrounding him, with my Fuda in hand, and waited for a moment until he was free.

I said, with a bow, "Excuse me, Honorable Master, would you stamp my Fuda?"

He replied gruffly, "*Chotto matte* (just a minute)."

I waited a few minutes until he disgorged himself from the crowd of people. Then stealthily he approached me.

His voice became mild as he said, "How may I help you?"

I responded, "I would appreciate a temple seal on my Fuda."

He seemed a little more accommodating, "Very well let us go over to my desk."

I followed his shuffling feet across the room until we reached a small table on which were a stamp pad and a seal. He then took my Fuda and spread it on the table. With unusual deftness he impressed the red ink of the seal onto its proper spot.

He struck up a conversation, "I see this is your first day of traveling. How do you like it so far?"

I replied, "The scenery is beautiful but I am trying to meditate as I walk and find this very difficult."

He looked at me straight in the eye, "Meditation takes many forms but you will find the proper method eventually."

I inquired, "It is near the end of day. Do you know of a ryokan nearby?"

He answered, "Yes. A short distance down the road is the Ryokan Tsuburo. I am sure they will be able to accommodate you."

I said, "Thank you."

I bowed with hands together (Gassho) and took my leave after proper obeisance at the shrine and depositing several coins in the donation box. As I left the temple I noticed the sun, like a red ball, hanging on the western horizon. I walked down the road and after a while came upon the Ryokan Tsuburo. Well, not exactly. What I saw before me was a Japanese house with a shingled roof. It had an outside garden, bordered with flowers just before the entrance, through which I walked on a stone path. When I arrived I was met at the door by the *Okusan* (house mistress). I noticed she had the nose of a bird, thin lips, piercing eyes and a skin that was too delicate. The beauty of her moved me as did cut lilies wet with dew. I was thrilled at recognizing a breed that must have derived from a goddess and a bird.

I entered and removed my shoes. As it turned out this was not a Japanese Inn (Ryokan) but a Japanese house with guest rooms *(minshuku)*. Having exchanged greetings with the Okusan I put on the provided house slippers and followed her to my room. I ordered dinner since I had not eaten any thing but the two Fuji apples since breakfast. I bathed, washed my staff, and returned to my room to await my dinner meal.

The Okusan came with my meal on a tray. I could not believe my eyes. A meal fit for a king. It consisted of miso soup with tofu and wakame (misoshiro) as a starter; followed by Japanese chicken kebab (yakitori), Japanese salad (wafu) and rice balls (onigiri). This was all to be washed down with the usual warm and friendly pot of tea (ocha).

The interior of a Japanese house is so simple in its construction, and so unlike anything to which I am accustomed in the arrangement of details of the interiors in my country, that it is difficult to find terms of comparison in attempting to describe it. The first thing that impresses one on entering a Japanese house is the small size and low stud of the rooms. The ceilings are so low that in many cases one can easily touch them, and in going from one room to another one is apt to strike his head against the *kamoi*, or lintel. The rectangular shape of my room and the general absence of all jogs and recesses save the *tokonoma* and companion recess are noticeable features. The division between the recesses consists of a light partition partly closed, which separates the recesses into two equal bays. The bay nearest the verandah is called the *tokonoma.* In this recess is hanging a scroll picture, and on its floor, which is slightly raised above the level of the mats of the main floor, stands a vase with an ornamental flower structure (ikebana).

The companion bay has a little closet, which contains the futon. This is closed by sliding screens, and two shelves above, and also another long shelf near its ceiling, all closed by sliding screens. The outer screens of my room are covered with white paper, and when closed, a subdued and diffused light enters the room. There are no swinging doors anywhere. The floor is completely covered with straw mats, two or three inches in thickness. The absence of all furniture gave me an uninterrupted sweep of the floor. I unrolled and placed my futon on the floor and without ceremony or hesitation crawled in and fell fast asleep.

At 6:00 am the next morning the Okusan brought my breakfast, which consisted of boiled rice (*gohan*) with a raw egg yoke dressing the top. This was accompanied by a piece of vinegared fish (*kisu no sujime)* and a pot of tea. After finishing breakfast I bade goodbye to the Okusan and departed.

For the purpose of accurate travel, I have provided myself with a map compass for direction and a polar planimeter for mileage, which I use on the multiple maps I brought along. In looking at my map, my finger traced the route I would take: an oblique path across a two-mile stretch of desert to some small foothills at the mountain's base, along a gradually rising arched ridge running up the mountain's right flank, and onto some high cliffs that ringed the area below the summit like the collar of a shirt.

About a mile up the road, I took in the panorama and found that the air had turned chilly, packing a stiff breeze. An endless flower garden unfolded ahead speckled with the familiar coin-size flashes of brilliant orange, yellow, red, and blue. Butterflies were already in the air, taking advantage of the heat the sun could muster between the cold gusts. I am now on my way to the cluster of temples: Temple 72, Mandara-ji, Temple 73, Susshaka-ji, Temple 74, Koyama-ji, and Temple 75, Zentsu-ji near the city of Zentuji.

VI – MANDARA-JI

This area is known as the "heights". The heights are a lava plateau formed by volcanic eruptions. The plateau is itself a large flowerbed of over 1000 different kinds of plants – the lily of the valley in spring and the day lily in summer. The plateau is also dotted with lovely lakes and reminds me of Minneapolis in this regard. A river falls down through wild woods – sometimes in cascades, now in rapids and now settling in abysses. There are literally thousands of maple trees in the area. The image of colorful maple leaves reflected on the lake water and the quiet standing of the old Mandara-ji Temple are really symbolic of the beauty of Japan.

Nearly two hours later, after a grueling climb I arrived at Temple 72, Mandara-ji, perched in a murky light in an immense mountain valley surrounded by a few snowy peaks. A light breeze was blowing, and with a temperature near seventy degrees Fahrenheit, the basin was a vision of paradise. As far as the eye could see, the cradling mountains were steeped in an almost liquid blue that seemed to mask any sense of distance. Here and there, at indiscernible intervals, lights from surrounding villages appeared and then vanished in eerie, intermittent rhythms, perhaps caused by the movement of air, clouds, or trees.

The temple had the appearance of a chalet like hotel, but of course, this was only an illusion caused by the surroundings. It was, however, built in typical Japanese style with a tiled roof, ending in tiled eaves, and ornamental coping, wooden framework throughout and sitting on a stone walled foundation. Entrance to the temple meant going up a short flight of stone steps after first passing through a massively double- doored wooden gate *(Mon)*. The atmosphere inside was smoky and smelled of the sandalwood odor typical of Japanese incense.

As I walked inside I noticed the paucity of people. Perhaps the climb was too strenuous for the average person. The temple supervisor approached me with a hurried gait. He was an average size man, dressed in black robes and with a shaved head. As he started to talk to me, his facial muscles began to twitch, as if a smile were trying to climb on to his face, like a spider, against his will.

He spoke with a smile on his face, "Welcome, dear sir. May I help you?"

I responded with a bow, "Good day, Reverend. Could you please stamp my Fuda?"

I handed him my rolled up Fuda and followed him to a table where he unrolled it and stamped the proper spot with the typical red ink of the temple seal.

In a state of mild exhaustion, I said, "Thank you. May I rest here for a few moments?"

Life is more than a series of moments

"Yes, Indeed", he responded. "Please allow me to introduce you to another traveler over at the wall."

He pointed to a young man sitting splay-legged on the floor with his back to the wall and his head hanging sideways like a doll's.

"Good day. My name is Shansky. May I join you?"

"Yes, of course. Please sit. My name is Hoda."

He spoke perfect English and extended his hand in western fashion. It was then I noticed something strange about his face. It was round and full like a westerner but his eyes were definitely Mongoloid. He had long unruly hair and a stubble of beard concentrated at his chin. His nose was big and full like most westerners.

"My full name is Hoda Miller. My mother is Japanese and my father was American. I was born in Kyoto but lived most of my life in Takamatsu. I am glad to meet you."

In mild curiosity I asked, "Are you on the henro pilgrimage?"

"No, not really. I hike up to the "heights" occasionally to get away from city life. How about you?"

"Yes. I am on the henro."

"No. I mean; where are you from and what do you do?"

"I'm from Connecticut in the USA. I came to Japan or more particularly to Shikoku to do the henro pilgrimage."

Then suddenly he seemed embarrassed by the next question.

"Are you a Buddhist?"

In a straightforward way I answered, "No, but I subscribe to most of the Buddhist principles. How about you; are you a Buddhist?"

He held his head down as he answered, "I don't know. My father was a Mormon missionary and my mother is a Shingon Buddhist."

I casually remarked, "You speak English remarkably well."

He answered with charming lilt in his voice, "My father always spoke to me in English and my mother always spoke to me in Japanese, even though each could speak both languages."

"I see. That is very interesting. Are your parents nearby?"

He seemed somewhat morose as he explained, "My father died some years ago. My mother and I live in the same house in Takamatsu."

Being curious I asked, "What did you mean by "I don't know" when you responded to my question about being a Buddhist?"

He lifted his head and looked at me, "My father, as a missionary, spent his entire life trying to convert the local Japanese to Christianity. He was more or less successful with many people but he failed with my mother and me. It was on the rare occasion that we would accompany him to the Chapel but there was always tension under these circumstances."

"Did you say tension?"

"Yes. My mother always felt that being Japanese required her loyalty to a Japanese religion. She always felt that Christianity was foreign and anathema to her lifestyle. I was able to digest much of both religions but never formally converted or adopted either one.

For this reason, I don't know if I am a Christian or a Buddhist. Now! Tell me about yourself."

I began a short litany, "Well, I was born a Jew but I never was very religious. I have many doubts about God; his usefulness and his existence. I learned a lot about Buddhism through my avid interest in Oriental art. I dabbled with Buddhism for a while when traveling to Minneapolis on business. I attended some rituals and spoke with some people on occasion at the Minnesota Zen Center on Lake Calhoun in Minneapolis. I was influenced greatly by the concept of self-reliance. Other than that I have no more connection to Buddhism than you; probably less. But I would like to add that I have made many trips to Japan both for business and pleasure and am very familiar with Japanese culture."

He seemed interested in continuing the questioning.
"How do you feel about religion?"

A strange thing about religion is that we all know
what it is until someone asks us to tell them.

I broke out in a broad smile. "Was it Karl Marx who said religion is the opiate of the masses? If you analyze that statement you find that religion is of value to some people, particularly the deprived, disadvantaged, and downtrodden. It gives them hope in their misery by enlisting the aid of a super being through entreaty."

He looked at me quizzically. "Isn't that true for westerners only? After all Buddhism and Daoism are religions without a Supreme Being. Christians, for example, find spiritual solace and satisfaction through faith and prayer in and to an anthropomorphic God. Buddhism, derisively called an atheistic religion by some, asks you to reach inwardly to the God within you."

I hastened to respond, "What you say is true and it is that aspect of Buddhism that I am exploring. It is said that Buddhism is a self-reliant religion. Do you believe that?"

He looked up as he spoke. "Yes, I do. But it is very difficult to rely on a weak character. Religion requires strong support which can only come from a quixotic imagery; hence a God."

I said goodbye to Hoda with a hearty handshake. I then bowed at the shrine and took my leave by the doorway. It was a beautiful day and I knew I would have much time to reflect on my conversation with Hoda during my upcoming trek. I now had to find my way to Temple 73, Susshaka-ji.

But first, I wanted to make another side trip. This time I went to Kotohira. Kotohira is home of the Kompira Shrines, which rank second only to the Grand Shrines of Ise in the amount of veneration accorded them. An hour's climb to the summit of Mt. Zozu above Kompira is tiring but well worth it for the spectacular view over the Inland Sea. I was now in a hyperborean way but I enjoyed the view nevertheless. I knew I would be descending soon.

VII – SUSSHAKI-JI

As I walked into the bright sunshine I noticed before me the teeming meadows of wildflowers. I began strolling downhill in a state of euphoria. Suddenly, unannounced, a cloudburst came out of nowhere, covering the road with so much mud it was nearly impossible to distinguish it from the surrounding flats. I was drenched from head to toe and felt like a wet noodle. Walking was becoming difficult and arduous slogging in the mud. Not only was I wet but I began sweating profusely making life most strenuous. After the deluge stopped, almost as suddenly as it began, the road was awash with water, rocks, and small boulders, making it nearly impossible to keep going. The hairs-on-neck prickliness has made me a cautious hiker. I never lost the sense that some awful disaster was lurking just around the corner.

My spirits were dampened but I decided to sit on a boulder and wait it out until the roadway improved. Spying a Japanese woman with a bright red hat and a basket walking with two children, I asked the way to Susshaka-ji. She did not answer, hurrying along, but it seemed to me, looking into the distance far ahead there appeared the outline of a small village, which shouldn't take more than fifteen minutes to reach. Finally, after slogging my way, I came upon a cluster of empty, abandoned houses of a ghostly village. The latch on the sheet-metal door of one of the huts had been broken off.

Though cold and anxious and with much trepidation I entered the hut, swathed in my muddied clothes and discovered an empty room completely void of furniture but with a large cement tub in the far corner. I approached the tub cautiously and curiously as if examining a gift. On opening the spigot, to my utter surprise, clean, cold water flowed and splashed like manna from heaven. I clapped my hands in childlike delight. I immediately undressed and crawled up into the tub to wash myself. I washed by sitting on my knees in an uncomfortable position but was able to affect a satisfactory outcome.

Dripping wet, I left the tub and began washing my clothes free of the accumulated mud, grime and dirt. When I finished I walked outside, completely naked, carrying the bundle of rinsed clothes to dry in the sun. By now the sun was approaching high temperatures and I had no doubt that they would dry quickly. I tried to squeegee the water off my body with the palms of my hands. After a restless waiting period, I decided to put on the partially dried and damp clothes fearful that someone might come by and embarrass me.

I decided to consult my map again because I had no idea where I was. Naturally, the map contained no information regarding the ghost town that I was in. After some deliberation, I decided to head northwest. Moving into the lush uplands, however, I found that the steep slopes and capricious weather made walking difficult. Currents driven from the ocean encounter the intermontane air, a collision that results in a tumultuous mix of sun, mist, and fog that can change within minutes. I proceeded downward, the sun would suddenly burn through the clouds, for a while transforming the surroundings into a hot house. By now my clothes dried on my body and I felt a lot more comfortable. As I reached the lowland I discovered a road, which matched one on my map. I elected to take this road towards the western coastline.

The weather was now tolerable and, of course, walking became easier. The road then turned and headed south. In a few minutes of walking, I could hear the roar of traffic coming from the Takamatsu Expressway and I knew I was going in the right direction. By a startling stroke of luck there it was up ahead. I could see Temple 73, Susshaka-ji. It looked almost like a mirror image of Mandara-ji, what is known in chemistry as a chiral.

A spacious lawn and well-kept flower gardens surrounded the temple. I walked up to the entrance on a winding, dirt path. As I entered and removed my shoes, the temple supervisor with several low bows and mutterings greeted me. He was an extremely short man, no more than five feet. He wore the traditional black robes and had the usual shaved head. His face was gaunt with high cheekbones and extremely slanty eyes, which almost hid his pupils. He looked like he hadn't eaten for a week. Coming from his upper lip and chin was a thin, stringy, flowing mustache and goatee, which made him look like Fu Manchu.

He greeted me in a pleasant tone and with kind words.

"Welcome, friend. You look like you have come from the "heights". Have you been to Mandara-ji?"

"Yes. I got caught in a downpour and had to wash up at a ghost town."

"Oh yes, I know the place. The ghost town, as you call it, was originally established many years ago as a cooperative farming community by some idealists but due to several years of extremely dry weather they all left and it was abandoned. Now it houses wanderers and ascetics."

With some curiosity I asked, "By idealists, do you mean it was a utopian community?"

"I believe so. Come, you look tired, let us have some tea. You are the first pilgrim to come today. Let us chat as you rest."

I followed him to a small room behind the shrine wherein a metal teapot with boiling water was on a small portable stove. He made the tea in large stoneware mugs, which had no handles and offered one to me as he started the conversation with a question.

"Tell me, dear sir, is there a soul?"

Life is an onion which one peels in tears.

As is said in Latin, *brevi docebo,* I shall briefly tell.

"Early Hebraic accounts of the person were holistic and there was no well-developed account of life after death. By Jesus' day, however, it was debated as to whether or not the dead would rise at the end of time. Jews had adopted a dualistic view of body and soul, along with a conception of the soul's survival after death. But there is no explicit teaching on the metaphysical composition of a person."

"Is this believed by all western religions?"

"My focus was on Judaism but there are important parallels with Christianity and to some extent with Islam. All western religions are substantial, that is, they believe in a fixed and unchanging God. Therefore, they are dualistic – God and Satan, good and bad, and body and soul."

"I see. Buddhism is non-dualistic. It believes that evil is a part of goodness; that you cannot have good without bad. But tell me what the soul is? Please explain."

"Plato, in early 400 BCE, taught that the soul is incorporeal and eternal, pre-existing the body. Plato described the person as an immortal soul imprisoned in a mortal body. Plato's concept of the soul was related to his "other-worldly" view of reality. During much of his career he held the doctrine of the *Forms or Ideas* – the view that concepts have a real existence and are eternal. He argued that, since people possess knowledge of these concepts or *Forms* without being taught them, they must come to know them by acquaintance before birth. Thus, the rational part of the soul pre-exists the body, dwelling in the transcendent realm of the *Forms*, and returns there after death."

"Do all westerners believe this?"

"Pope John Paul II reaffirmed the compatibility of evolutionary biology with Catholic teaching with the statement that "if the human body takes its origin from pre-existent living matter, the spiritual soul is immediately created by God." This affirms a dualist account of the human person."

"I see. But ancient Buddhism recognized that all composite things are devoid of an essence (anatman); that is empty of self-nature. It does not mean that things do not exist but rather that they are nothing besides appearances, and are without duality and empirical forms."

"So, Buddhists do not believe in the existence of a soul or a self."

"No, they do not."

"I am most grateful for this moment to converse with you. But now I must be off to continue my odyssey. Would you please stamp my Fuda before I leave?"

He bowed and took my Fuda from my proffered hands and stamped the temple seal in the designated spot.

"May your journey be easy and a lifetime usufruct, dear sir. I too enjoyed our time together."

I left with the distinct feeling that he had performed this type of conversation with other foreigners many times previously. I bowed to the Buddha at the shrine, placed several coins in the donation box and walked into the sunshine heading for the next temple.

After consulting my map I noticed that, for some unknown reason, Temple 75, Zentsu-ji came first. I, therefore, decided to do that temple first then go on to Temple 74, Koyama-ji next and afterwards spend the night in the town of Zentuji.

I was now heading in a northward direction along a relatively improved road. Occasionally, a small pick-up truck or an automobile would pass me as I trudged along. Then I saw a roadside stand (*shokuryohinya*) selling foodstuffs of various sorts. I decided to eat *alfresco*, the exotic and down-home street specialties; so I bought a *bento* (a box lunch), which contained three large shrimp tempura, several rice balls and mixed vegetables with shitake mushrooms and a container of cold tea. I sat on a makeshift bench outside in front of the shop and enjoyed the warmth of the sun while I ate. I could hear the portamento of a bird singing like the clarinet solo in Gershwin's Rhapsody in Blue. Despite the problems resulting from the previous downpour experience, I decide to lift up my heart as in a *sursum corda* and go on with renewed courage.

VIII – ZENTSU-JI

After my little respite was over I was off again on the road. That's when I saw an immense bird, which I took to be a fish-hawk; this was a large bird, of high and rapid flight; his wings are very long and pointed, and he spreads a vast sail, in proportion to the volume of his body. This princely bird subsists entirely on the fish, which he takes himself. Waterfowl and the various species of land-birds also abound. Walking along this road, which paralleled the seacoast, gave me access to this delightful array of sea birds. I wandered along a little farther among the evergreens of the area.

The native Pitch Pine is the only tree that will grow in some of the windswept sections of Shikoku. Whether or not any truly wild larches survive in the area is difficult to determine, but I have not found any such native larches growing along the roadside where you would expect to find them.

I suddenly discovered to my surprise that there was a Praying Mantis on the shoulder of my jacket. To my great relief, I removed it from its perch and wrapped it loosely in a handkerchief for transportation to a more appropriate feeding ground. This fierce-looking insect is really harmless to everything except the other insects on which it feeds.

If a special heaven were designed for walkers to go to when they die, it would have to be modeled on the island of Shikoku. Here there is everything; here nature and man have lived together for centuries in such gentle harmony that to my eyes, at least, it seems that no violence has been done to either.

In an hours' stroll I was able to anticipate the image of the Temple 75, Zentsu-ji. This could not come too soon for me because I was aware of being footsore and leg weary. Even so, I learned that muscles strengthen, feet toughen and I found walking could be a pleasure. I released the Praying Mantis on a long blade of grass and resumed my walk to the temple. I sort of stumbled into the temple due to my tired condition. I needed a place to sit.

I saw the temple supervisor rushing over to me. He was an unusually tall man for Japanese, taking long strides and as he approached me with outstretched arms I felt the warmth of his welcome.

"Please, dear sir, sit over here by the wall. You look very tired."

With a bow I said, "Thank you, Reverend; I've had a hard day."

He stretched out his hand. "Let me have your Fuda while you are resting and I shall stamp it with the temple seal."

I opened my shoulder bag, removed the rolled up Fuda and gave it to him. He took it and departed for a while. As I sat, my eyes leisurely roamed the temple room *(hatto)*. Getting used to the light, I began to notice several other people; a mix of older men and women dressed in the authentic white Henro garb, which apparently is the touchstone of the pilgrimage. The temple supervisor returned with the Fuda in one hand and a bunch of what appeared to be a large cluster of grapes in the other.

"Here is your Fuda. I brought you a bunch of lichees for your eating pleasure."

He handed me the Fuda, which I retrieved with one hand and I accepted the bunch of lichees with the other hand.

"Thank you Reverend you are most kind."

I put the rolled-up Fuda in my shoulder bag and began to look quizzically at the woody, horny covering on the fruit.

He approached with outstretched hand. "Let me show you how to eat them."

He plucked one round fruit from the tendrils and pressed the skin covering back with both thumbs revealing a white, round fruit inside swimming in a sweet, colorless fluid. He handed it to me and I quickly mouthed the juicy, white fruit. It was deliciously sweet, piquant, and racy. I crushed the fruit between my tongue and palate and removed the pit from my mouth. It seemed to give me virile strength and vigor. I ate the remaining six succulent lichees off the tendrils with eagerness and vitality.

It tasted like pure ambrosia. It was my first experience with such an exotic fruit.

I licked my lips and shook my head affirmatively.

"I'm glad you enjoyed it."

"Thank you, most kindly, Reverend. I feel rested and refreshed now."

I got up and after putting the spent tendrils and pits in my pocket I walked to the shrine where I lit three incense sticks and bowed to the Buddha three times. I placed the incense sticks in the censor amongst the others and noticed that there was an offering bowl of pyramidal arranged oranges. As I stepped back I was aware that people were eyeing me and I assumed it was due to my disheveled state. My appearance was certainly out of character.

I deposited several coins in the donation box and was about to leave when I noticed the temple supervisor with a broad smile on his fleshy face, waving to me. I could not forget his kindness and so I approached him with a *Gassho* (palms together) and a low bow by way of deep respect.

"Goodbye Reverend; be well and thank you once again."

I left Temple 75, Zentsu-ji and headed for Temple 74, Koyama-ji. The road was smooth and relatively easy to traverse. Heading north, I once again noticed the plethora of different kinds of birds amongst the treetops. This outdoor exploration and brief excursion really put me in touch with nature. I have always been interested in wildlife and so feel particularly fortunate to have had the opportunity of this walk.

IX – KOYAMA-JI

I passed scattered farmhouses and patches of tilled ground as I made my way northward. My map showed many brooks and streams that ran from high ground on the island in a zigzag course into the rivers, which eventually emptied into the ocean. I then came to a bridge, which crossed over one branch of a creek for north and south travel. Suddenly, a family of ungulates strolled nearby but the deer scampered off into the trees after they saw me. I was thrilled by this encounter and hoped for the sight of more animals that might wander about the area. Along the roadway a view upland revealed flowering shrubs, which appeared to be a Japanese version of mountain laurel on the hillside. These colorful flowers dotted the hillside with a pointillist effect.

I was impressed with the different kinds of small mammals I saw in the meadows, particularly the Meadow Mice, who would dart in and out of their burrows. A great day, indeed!

The ridge is still high on the road as I approached the temple, which stands on solid rock. Autoists on the Takamatsu Expressway see the exposed western face of this formation as a sheer cliff overhanging the motor parkway. The rock formation remains high far to the south from whence I came.

Temple 74, Koyama-ji stands high on the ground as one approaches it. The architecture is typical Japanese with a roof-line that exhibits the flowing tiles to best advantage. The temple is surrounded by a large flower garden, which is made more pronounced by the inclusion of various odd shaped rocks. I walked through this garden on a winding stone path until I reached the temple entrance. Placing my shoulder bag on the floor, I removed my shoes and noticed several people milling about – some in Henro uniform.

I walked inside with a bow and Gassho to several of the people I met. I immediately saw the temple supervisor – whom I recognized by his black robes and shaved head. As I approached, I saw that he was an older man with a craggy face and neck and gray eyebrows sprouting over his eyes like a sheep dog. He had very thin lips, which were drawn over in a half-moon shape. He had no obvious facial hair.

"Good day, Reverend." I said with a bow and gassho.

"Good day to you, dear sir."

"Your garden is very beautiful." I said with enthusiasm.

"Thank you. I tend to it myself."

"I notice more people here than in Temple Zentsu-ji."

He looked around then commented, "Well, I think that's because there is a temple nearby up the road associated with us. It is called *Senyugahara jizo-do. Jizo* is the child-daishi or the child protector. People come here from long distances to pray on behalf of their children. The deity of our temple is *Yakushi* even though we are of the Shingon sect and one would expect Kobo Daishi or Kannon to be the deity.

In the Book of Proverbs there is a whole network of sayings relating to the proper instruction of children

"Did you say Yakushi?"

"Yes. *Yakushi-bhaisajya-guru* Buddha is known as the Buddha of Healing or the Medicine Buddha. Some people who have maladies come here to pray for healing and good health.

"Thank you for the explanation. I wonder if you could please stamp my Fuda with the temple seal."

"I would be happy to have that honor. Where are you going from here?"

"I think I will go to the town of Zentuji and look for a hotel."

"There is only one hotel there; it is called Zentuji Hotel."

He laughed as he stamped my Fuda and returned it to me.

I suddenly felt the urge to defecate and asked permission to use the *benjo* (toilet). He directed me to a free standing room attached to the back of the temple. I entered the room and saw a typical Japanese toilet, which is basically a china bowl in squat position placed in the floor. The space was partially illuminated as in a penumbra and there was no possibility of sitting. Squatting is a very uncomfortable position for westerners but Japanese men and women use this position all the time without complaint. Indeed, all Asians learn to squat on their haunches from childhood on.

X - ZENTUJI

After taking care of my "biology", I continued back down the road to the town of Zentuji. I retraced much of my steps until I came to a fork in the road leading to the northeast. If one stands, as I did, on a high spot on a clear day and looks to the northeast, a mountain range is visible in the distance. The undulating mountains are silhouetted against a bright glow in the eastern sky. The road eventually became much more improved and after a while was busy with traffic going to the town of Zentuji.

When I reached the outskirts of town, which was somewhat hidden in the mountains, I immediately made inquiry as to the location of the hotel. Many people were helpful and I soon found myself walking on "civilized" streets with sidewalks. Zentuji is actually a basin encircled by mountains. The surrounding mountains are not very high, the tallest peaks rising about 3000 feet above sea level. They are, however, quite steep, and the fast-running rivers have cut deep valleys into them. The mountains have always protected Zentuji, from military invasion in feudal times and from large-scale industrialization over the past several decades. Its relative isolation has helped preserve a rich legacy of folklore and traditions. Although little known to the general public, Japanese or foreigners, folklorists and anthropologists recognize Zentuji as a treasure house.

There one can still see, for example, an old woodcutter who, before cutting a tree, prays to the god of the mountain for permission to take something from the deity's domain. Shrines and temples dedicated to deities of Buddhism, Shinto, and folk belief dot the landscape. However, the magic of the Zentuji basin remains. The folds of its many mountains enclose places and people imbued with the spirit of old Japan. There can be seen verdant valleys, clear-flowing streams, and villages snuggled in the woods. Pilgrims, such as me, hike from temple to temple, greeted by weathered stone statues that have stood for hundreds of years.

As I walked the streets of Zentuji I passed the JR Station and immediately came upon the local business district. I noticed stores of various types such as a green grocer, a bank, a photo shop, a sweets shop, and a department store. Across the street from the department store was the Hotel Zentuji. It looked to be the tallest building in town. The front was decorated in a bright and lively red and yellow paint.

A young, uniformed girl opened the front door for me, who bowed. I entered and approached the front desk. There in front of me was a young man dressed in a dark blue business suit. He looked up in an innocent diffident manner, adjusted his glasses and greeted me.

"How may I help you?"

"Do you have a room for me?"

"Yes. How long will you stay?"

"Two nights." I answered.

I have already decided to rest for two days in town before continuing my journey. My map showed the distances between Temple 76 and 77 to be about fifteen miles and between Temple 77 and 78 to be about twenty miles and between Temple 78 and 79 to be about twenty miles. The temples are no longer in clusters. They are laid out in linear fashion along the coastline in a northeast to easterly direction back towards Takamatsu.

"May I have your passport while you register?"

"Certainly."

"The room has a private bath; will that be suitable?"

"Does it have a hot tub for soaking?"

"Indeed, it does. I shall have the maid fill it and put the temperature on automatic."

"That will be fine. It is getting late now and I noticed a restaurant off the lobby. Is it open for dinner?"

"Yes. It's open now."

"The maid can attend to the tub while I eat dinner. I also want to have my clothes washed and pressed."

"There is a laundry bag in your room. Put all your clothes in the bag and leave it outside your room this evening and it will be ready in the morning."

"Thank you."

I left the front desk and went upstairs by elevator to my room. Opening the door I found a very small room with a large western bed. I put my bag down and washed my hands and face as well as my walking stick in the bathroom. I then went down to a very needy dinner. I was famished. I ordered dinner from the menu, which had a picture of the dishes. It was called *Teppan-yaki* and consisted of fried lotus root *(age renkon),* grilled meat and vegetables *(teppan-yaki)*, string beans with goma sauce *(ingen no goma-ae)*, and okra miso soup *(okura no misoshiro)* as well as a bowl of boiled rice *(gohan)* and a pot of tea *(ocha)*.

I found myself wolfing down the food. I was eating too fast, which could result in indigestion. I slowed down and ate leisurely to enjoy this culinary delight. After dinner I went back to my room, removed all of my clothes and put them in the laundry bag and placed it outside my room. I then went into the bathroom and sat on the small wooden bench and soaped myself with a lovely scented soap. I finally showered off all the lather and entered the hot tub. The water was very inviting. I tried stretching out as far as I could but my legs had to be folded beneath me because the tub was very small. I just let my body relax in a suspended state for a few minutes until I found myself dozing off. I then removed myself from the tub, dried with a large towel, put on the provided *yukata* (cotton robe) and got into bed. I do not remember falling asleep.

I awoke at 6:00 am and realized that I had slept twelve hours. I opened my door and found a package outside containing my clothes – washed and ironed and packaged in flat condition. I immediately showered, shaved and brushed my teeth. Then I put on my clean clothes and reveled in a restored spirit. And so with a renewed vigor I left the room in search of breakfast. When I arrived in the lobby I noticed the dining room was open. I decided to go in and inspect the menu. Sitting for a while trying to decipher the list of available dishes I was approached by a tall man wearing a completely white, immaculate uniform with a tall white hat sitting on his head. He was obviously a chef of sorts.

"Good morning, Gaijin (foreigner). Did you sleep well?"

"Good morning. Yes, I slept twelve hours. I must have been very tired. It is the first time I slept in a bed since I came to Japan. I usually sleep in a futon."

"Are you from *Beikoku* (America)?"

"Yes. I am an American."

"Would you like a real treat this morning for breakfast?"

"What do you mean?"

"I can make you an authentic English breakfast. You see I was a chef in a British Army Officers Club in Bombay and learned to cook in the English manner."

"Well that would be very nice. Thank you."

He departed with a shake of his head and a broad grin on his face. I just sat and looked around at the people. They averted my eyes when I connected with them, in some sort of embarrassment. After a while the chef returned followed by a waitress who carried a tray of comestibles.

"Here it is; fried kippers, two fried eggs and bacon, with toast and marmalade and a pot of Earl Gray English tea."

I was surprised beyond words.

"This is wonderful. How did you do it?"

"The kippers and bacon sold in packages and are available in the food section of the department store across the street, called the B1. Kippers are becoming popular in Japan. Of course, they are eaten with boiled rice."

"Well, this is wonderful. Thank you very much."

"May I ask when you are leaving Zentuji?"

"I shall be continuing my Henro at Temple 76 tomorrow morning."

"What good fortune! I am going to that area to the fish market on the coast. Would you like a ride? But, I am leaving early at 4:30 am."

"Yes, indeed. 4:30 will be fine. Where shall we meet?"

"Meet me in front of the Hotel. I'll be driving a gray Toyota pick-up truck."

After finishing breakfast I went into the street to scout about. I really enjoy seeing all sides of Japan and city life reveals a new dimension to my travels.

To have a passion for something is the greatest happiness on earth.

Seeing the department store before me I crossed the street only to find that it was closed until 9:00 am. I decided such a visit would be an otiose venture having seen such department stores in other Japanese cities. I strolled along until I came upon a bakery *(panya)*. I could not read the Japanese characters *(kanji)* on the sign but one look in the window convinced me that it was a bakery featuring western cakes and cookies. A lady emerge from the inside carrying what looked like a baguette or a French bread. She offered it to me.

"This is our first attempt at baking western bread. We would like you to have it as our gift."

I was stunned by this generosity and could only respond with faint praise and labored acknowledgement. She invited me in and wrapped the bread in paper. I purchased a cream puff and praised its quality even though it was not really as good as I am used to.

"I wish you much luck with your venture into western breads. Do the Japanese people eat much bread?"

"Yes, western bread is becoming more popular, especially with children who enjoy eating sandwiches. We think bread making will be a good business opportunity for us since we are doing well with cakes. My husband learned to bake western style in a bakery in Tokyo."

"Thank you once again. I shall eat the bread for lunch. Goodbye and good luck."

I left the bakery carrying the gift of bread and continued my scouting. It was too early in the morning to find any stores open so I just wandered until I came to a park. I sat on a bench and enjoyed my surroundings in peace and tranquility. After a while the silence was broken by the laughter and screams of children. Apparently there was a school on the other side of the park, which had just let the children out for recess. I walked over to watch them and discovered that they played at the same games as the children at home. One of the teachers came over to the fence where I was standing and began talking to me in perfect English.

"Good morning. Are you a stranger in town?"

"Yes. I am on the Henro pilgrimage and I am leaving early tomorrow."

"Are you American?"

"Yes. I live in Connecticut."

"Oh, I know where that is. I went to college in New York City for a while. It was called Hunter College."

"Yes, I know Hunter. Are you a teacher here?"

"Yes, I teach sixth grade. I must go now but I enjoyed speaking with you."

I suspected that she was just practicing her English. There are probably very few opportunities to do so. I wandered on until I came to a Shinto shrine. After I passed under the *Torii* gate I came to the shrine building, which had a large, dull bell to ring with a hanging knotted cord. There was a statue of a horse nearby and this reminded me that Shinto is an animistic religion.

It was characteristic of the religious views of the ancient Japanese that they believed spirits to reside in all kinds of things. They personified all kinds of spirits other than those of human beings, considering them all as ancestral gods, and tending to view every spirit as a divine ghost. It is such a turn of thought that gave birth to the Shinto shrines, for in order to perform religious ceremonies the gods and spirits were fixed in certain specified places. The most primitive form of this practice consists in the invocation and worship of spirits in some specific natural object, e.g., mountain, river, forest, tree, or stone. Forms of worship of ancient times were generally of this character; even today there remain shrines that are pantheistic of this type.

Many Japanese people belong to both Buddhist and Shinto temples, since both religions have learned to meld with each other. For example, they marry by a Shinto Priest and are buried by a Buddhist Priest. I left the Shinto Shrine and wandered leisurely back to the hotel. I went to my room where I ate the whole bread with the provided tea for lunch. It was really good. Having eaten lunch I decided to go out again for the afternoon busy time.

On the streets I found many women shopping by bicycle placing their purchases in a basket over the front wheel. They would stop occasionally and converse with each other. There was a minimal amount of auto traffic in town and most noticeable the streets and sidewalks were extremely clean. I passed many shops until I came to the bank where I changed a 1000-yen note for twenty 50-yen coins to be used in donation boxes at temples. At the end of the day after mindless wandering, I returned to the hotel for an early dinner. In the restaurant I ordered Udon with chicken *(nikomi udon)*, which is made with Udon noodles, Bonito soup, flavored with Mirin and soy sauces and spinach, carrots, onions, and shitake mushrooms.

When I finished my dinner I paid my hotel bill with my credit card then I returned to my room, read for a while, set my clock for 4:00 am and went to bed. I awoke at 4:00 am, showered, shaved and dressed. I grabbed my shoulder bag, my walking stick and went downstairs. The chef was waiting for me at the front entrance of the hotel.

"Good morning, honorable chef. How are you?"

"Good morning, Gaijin. Shall we be off?"

"My name is Shansky. What is your name?"

"My name is Hideko. Have you eaten breakfast?"

"No. I haven't."

"I thought not; so I brought some fish cakes along. Have some please."

I partook of the basket containing the brown fish cakes. They were delicious. Hideko rode out of town rapidly and we got to the main road without meeting any traffic. Soon we came to the road, which I had traversed on my way into Zentuji. The road was rocky and had some potholes, which caused the pick-up to lurch and bump. It was a pleasant morning when we reached the intersection where I bade goodbye to Hideko.

I went on afoot until I came to the cliff. This is a 300- foot cliff formed by a number of pillar-shaped rocks. I could hear the raging waves from the sea beating against the rugged rocks. By moonlight there is no comparable scenery like this along the coastlines of Shikoku.

XI – KOYZO-JI

When I reached the plateau, I found it to have one of the most hospitable climates in the world, with a mild temperature and as the sun rose there was a hint of a brilliant blue sky dotted with fair-weather cumulus clouds. Temple 76, Koyzo-ji sits at an altitude of about 300-feet and its site is strewn with low growing vegetation and grasses. It was 5:00 am and still somewhat dark and murky as I approached the heavy wooden door of the temple with trepidation. My flashlight revealed the door to be closed but I was able to push it open slowly. The temple supervisor was inside lighting candles and preparing the shrine. He turned to face me as his voice echoed.

"Welcome. I am about to begin meditation. Would you like to join me?"

I was startled for a moment but responded, "Yes, I would very much."

He turned from his work to advise me, "Well then light an incense stick. It will burn for forty minutes and that will time your involvement in meditation."

He then left and brought out of a rear closet a two- foot by three-foot mat and a round cushion.

As he placed them on the floor he said, "I think you would be most comfortable with these. I shall meditate in *seiza* position."

He then relaxed on his knees with a straight back, looking ahead at the Buddha with his hands together in a Gassho gesture. At this point I noticed his face bathed in candlelight giving the appearance of *chiaroscuro* reminiscent of the Georges de la Tour painting of two people on each side of a central candle. His face seemed to be afflicted with roseacea and his nose was bulbous like a proboscis monkey but blistered and puckered. He had a pleasant, winning smile, which showed his teeth spaced like a white picket fence.

I, on the other hand, after lighting the incense sat on the cushion with my right foot on my left thigh in a half lotus position. My hands were folded on each other in my lap with the thumbs touching and with the palm of the top hand as if carrying an egg. My eyes were half open. I learned this meditation procedure, called *Zazen*, in the Minnesota Zen Center. When the incense stick burned down, the temple supervisor hit a small bell, which resided on a cushion, with a hand clapper. He then began to chant in Japanese.

The chants and hymns *(Shomyo)*, which accompany Buddhist ritual, are of Chinese origin. Certain items are known to have reached Japan via Korea and to have been sung in the great Nara temples during the 7th and 8th centuries. The principal traditions of Buddhist chant, however, have always been those of the Tendai and Shingon sects, both founded in the early 9th century by monks who had studied in China.

When he finished chanting, which took about ten minutes he turned to me and asked:

"Did you have breakfast?"

"Well, I ate two fish cakes on the way from Zentuji."

"Would you like some tea?"

"Yes, indeed."

By this time my calves were aching and I felt an unconscious tremor in my thighs. I slowly got up with a Gassho and a bow to the Buddha. I then picked up the mat and cushion and returned them to the closet. Following the temple supervisor to a room behind the shrine I discovered a small table with two chairs; on the table was a hot plate containing a metal pot of boiling water.

He made two cups of tea and began to speak by asking questions of me.

"Tell me dear sir are you a Buddhist?"

I hesitated for a moment but said rather frankly," I have never actually joined a Buddhist organization but I enjoy Buddhist teachings and philosophy."

"You are on the Henro pilgrimage; does that mean you are interested in Shingon Buddhism?"

"Not really. When I first encountered Buddhism in America it was through a Zen group."

"Do you believe that one could become a Buddha in his lifetime?"

I looked down pensively as I responded, "I don't know."

He then became pedantic in his response, "Kukai, the founder of the Shingon sect said that one could not only become a Buddha in this world, but also that one could become a Buddha through ascetic practice during one's lifetime."

"Do you really believe that, honorable master?"

He continued his response, "This worldliness was plainly expressed by Kukai, the founder of the Japanese Shingon (True Word) sect. According to Kukai, the world and humanity both consist of six constituent elements, earth, water, fire, wind, sky, and intelligence. Their essence is the absolute truth, known as the World of the Law, and they are so perfectly interrelated as never to obstruct or oppose one another. It follows that mankind and Buddhas are identical in their essence. Kukai preached that if one should follow such reasoning, then making figures with one's hand, reciting incantations, or concentrating one's mind, which are the three actions of man's body, mouth, and mind, would be directly identified with those of a Buddha."

"Is that the so-called Doctrine of Esoteric Buddhism?"

"Yes. Kukai said: "One can attain the status of great enlightenment with the body that was born of one's parents.""

"Do Zen practitioners believe this also?"

"The this-worldly idea of becoming a Buddha alive in the body is also conspicuous in the Japanese Zen sect. Dogen, the founder of the Soto School, straightforwardly asserts that to attain enlightenment is not the function of the mind but that of the body."

141

I was silent for what seemed like a long time before answering, "Well, that's most interesting, but I must go now and continue my journey. Thank you for the tea and your views."

"Go in peace, dear sir. May your journey be kind and rewarding?"

I got up, bowed to the temple supervisor with a Gassho and left the temple after depositing a coin in the donation box. As I went through the door I heard the temple supervisor calling me.

"Sir, do you want your Fuda stamped?"

I realized I was leaving without having my Fuda stamped. On returning the temple supervisor was ready with the seal

"Thank you for reminding me," I said with some embarrassment.

"You are most welcome. Go in peace."

I walked outside and found the day beginning with bright sunshine and a mild temperature. I referred to my map and saw that by following the road in a northeasterly direction along the coastline I would reach Temple 77, Doryu-ji by noon. This road intermittently follows the Yosan JR Line, which I rode two days previously. It seems like a long time ago.

As I strolled along enjoying the salubrious weather, I could hear the waves of the sea beating against the rock formation of the Cliffside. Screeching sea birds were flying high over the water. The morning sun was high in the sky and over the next two hours I became completely absorbed in the actions of the birds. I remember being overwhelmed by the mystery of these birds, which in their calls and movements seemed to share some higher form of interspecific communication.

Coastal development forced shorebird concentrations into increasingly smaller areas until the government intervened and established protected reserves. Two such facilities on the pathway ahead are: Nakatsu Barishoen Park and Toryu Park. I hope to stop and explore them, if I have the time.

As I continued walking along this rather primitive road I spied, up ahead, a small creek flowing steadily and leisurely across the road, blocking passage. I had no choice but to remove my shoes and wade across. Leaving the creek, I struck off among a region of scoria buttes, the ground rising into rounded hills, through whose grassy covering the red volcanic rock showed in places, while boulder-like fragments of it were scattered all through the valleys between. There were a few clumps of bushes here and there, and near one of them were two magpies. Magpies are birds that catch the eye at once from their bold black-and-white plumage and long tails. They are very saucy and at the same time very cunning and shy.

Nowhere, not even at sea, does a man feel lonelier than when walking over the far-reaching, seemingly never-ending roads, their very vastness and loneliness and their melancholy monotony have a strong fascination for me.

> *When you're on a journey and the end keeps getting further and further away then you realize it is not the end but the journey that counts.*

In the words of the Sage of Concord, Ralph Waldo Emerson, the universe is composed of nature and the soul: "to go into solitude, a man needs to retire as much from chamber as from society, I am not solitary whilst I read and write, though nobody is with me. But if a man would be alone, let him look at the stars. The rays that come from those heavenly worlds will separate him and what he touches."

I remembered those words as I trudged along to Temple 77, Doryu-ji. The road is scorched to a dull brown and against its monotonous expanse any objects stand out with a prominence that makes it difficult to judge the distance at which they are. A mile or more off, I could see, through the strange shimmering haze, the shadowy white outlines of something, which looms vaguely up till it looks as large as the top of a building; but as I come nearer it shrinks and dwindles and takes clearer form until at last it changes into the edifice of the temple.

XII – DORYU-JI

I re-assumed my travels, proceeding down the high road, passing through a level country, well watered by large streams, branches of the rivers coursing from extensive swamps and marshes. These swamps are cleared and improved into large fruitful rice paddies and lentils fields. The road is straight, spacious, and kept in fairly good repair; and is generally bordered on each side with a light grove of trees and shrubs. I could see the extensive paddies and fields of rice and lentils, now in early verdure, decorated here and there with groves of floriferous and fragrant trees and shrubs.

Although the chief business of the Kanagawa prefecture is still agriculture, factories and tract housing are fast swallowing the grain fields around Takamatsu. Along with industrialization, the local authorities have welcomed mass commercial tourism. The horror of this landscape marring is too much for me to contemplate and ponder. Shikoku's most obvious enemy is the automobile, the trucks, buses and cars, which, here as elsewhere, jam the streets and shake the buildings of an earlier and gentler age. However, walking along this primitive road has enabled me to block out such thoughts of city life and strife.

By late morning, I reached Temple 77, Doryu-ji by the approach up an avenue of pine trees. Here a road of white sand leads to a gate, which dates from the year of the temple's construction. The temple's gently inclining roof and long eaves give it an air of stability and neatness.

On the left of the temple stands a pagoda. On a double stone foundation, it is so constructed that the width of the pillars on each of its five stories becomes gradually smaller by mathematical progression until the top story is only half the width of the bottom one. This device gives the building airiness and grace.

Walking into the main room *(hatto)* I noticed several pilgrims milling about while whispering in soft tones to each other. I bowed with a gassho as I passed each person. They were friendly but somewhat aloof. One older lady was eating a rice cake as she was strolling and offered the bag to me but I apologetically declined with a raised hand.

The temple supervisor was near the shrine surrounded by and speaking to a small group of pilgrims. He saw me and raised his gassho higher than expected as if in a recognizable gesture of acquaintance. Coming towards me I noticed he was rather young for a Buddhist priest; perhaps 25 or 30 years old. I immediately dismissed this thought as he greeted me.

"Good morning sir. How are you today?"

"I am fine honorable master."

"Have you come a long way?"

"I started the Henro at Temple 68. This is my third day of travel."

"Are you walking all the way?"

"Yes, I hope to do the whole Henro by walking."

"It may take you many weeks, but, by so doing, you will see all of Shikoku."

"Thank you. Would you please stamp my Fuda with the temple seal?"

"Of course, I would be most honored."

I followed him to a desk where he unrolled my Fuda and stamped the proper spot. He then rolled up the Fuda and handed it to me.

"Thank you, master."

"Please tell me, dear sir, are you an American?"

"Yes, I am."

"Oh, how very nice, I was a student for a while in Hanazono College in Kyoto. It was there I met several Americans who have remained my friends."

"Yes, I know the place. It's a Buddhist College, isn't it? Were the Americans training as Buddhist monks?"

"No, they were studying the Japanese language and literature."

"I see. I noticed a garden post outside with three Japanese characters in a vertical row. Can you tell me what it says? I cannot read Kanji."

"Yes. It says: Happy Land West."

"What does that mean?"

"Well, we are in Western Japan, eh, and that is a well-wishing greeting for people such as you who appear here."

"Oh, I see."

"How many temples each day do you visit?"

"Oh, about three, sometimes four, now, I must be on my way if I am to keep up that record. Thank you for your kindness, honorable master."

"Go in peace, dear American sir. Have a healthy and easy trip."

I lit three incense sticks at the shrine and bowed to the Buddha. Then, as I left, I deposited a coin in the donation box. Walking into the bright sunshine, I reflected on the possibility of this temple being a place of refuge for the young priest. I wish I could have learned more about him but as usual there is never enough time. I turned to look at the temple once more, beautifully decorated with gold, red and ochre paint, which is peeling a bit. Walking down the tree-lined avenue, I came to the white sand road, which sparkled in the sunlight and turned northeasterly for Temple 78, Gosho-ji. But first, due north from Doryu-ji is Nakatsu Barishoen Park, a stretch of rugged, but not very high country, covered with dense forest and containing some of the most magnificent views of Shikoku.

The entry to the park is just off the road, on which I am walking and enables me to traverse the park to the end and so leave to get back on the road. I found the entry through the park most interesting with its single main dirt road and its clear, invigorating air. It is a natural botanical garden but you can still get a feeling of really open space. The sweeping views over most of the park are breathtaking.

The alpine forest bursts with color and is so dense as to give it a primeval appearance. As I walked I noticed many people walking through the park; some with children; some looked like campers. I greeted them all with a gassho or a wave of the hand. They all greeted me in turn with friendly voices and gestures. Gazing a while on the park as I left, enabled me to saunter back to the road to continue my journey.

XIII – GOSHO-JI

It was a misty day in the late morning, and as I went up the road, the mist became heavier and heavier. One could hear the soft beat of drops of moisture on the leaves of grass. There was nothing to be seen but fog. My clothes were already half damp with the moisture. All about me was an expanse of mist and fog, with the outline of distant hills barely visible on the horizon. After a while I saw a large rock in the distance enveloped by the clouds, which had been heralded as a great sight. As I approached it, I thought it was an ugly marker of sorts, but in my present state, I guess, I haven't the heart to feel and the eyes to see.

Suddenly without warning, the sun broke through the clouds and the mist began to disappear. My mood changed immediately and I realized that I was hungry and tired; but where can I eat? My walk in the golden sunshine leads me to a great horse-chestnut tree, whose root offers a convenient seat in the shadow of its foliage. At that resting place I have no wide view before me, but what I see is enough – a corner of wasteland, over-flowered with poppies and charlock on the edge of a grain field. The charlock could be troublesome to the grain field. I am sure the farmers are aware of this.

The brilliant red and yellow colors harmonize with the glory of the day. Nearby, too, is a hedge covered with great white blooms of the bindweed? As soon as I renewed my being I stood up and straightened to re-assume my travel. By now, I had infinite energy, but not much muscular strength. I walked straight along the road when, unexpectedly, an automobile came along side, going in my direction. The driver stopped and popped his head out of the window.

"Good day to you, sir. May I give you a ride?"

I was taken aback by this greeting. "No, thank you. I am on the Henro pilgrimage and prefer to walk. But, do you know where I can get something to eat?"

"What luck, I have a large *bento* (box lunch) and would be glad to share it with you."

I was struck by this kindness. "That's very nice of you but I would not want to interfere with your lunch."

He responded very anxiously. "No, really, I can always get another bento in the next town. Why don't you take this bento with my compliments? I would be most honored for you to have it."

"Well, at least let me pay for it."

"Oh no, I wouldn't hear of it. It's not necessary. It is my privilege to help you."

He offered the bento through the car window. I reached up to take it while expressing my thanks.

"You are very kind to help me this way. I am very grateful and I wish for your life to be joyful and peaceful. Thank you once again."

I bowed to him with a deep gassho as he drove off waving his arm. I was struck by this moment of kindness and compassion. Reflecting with emotion on my past experiences with people encounters during this walk I find most to have been unusually kind and thoughtful. As I continued walking, I began looking for a suitable place to sit and have lunch. The sun was directly overhead and I mused that it must be the noon hour.

Finally, I found a small boulder at the roadside and decided to sit there for a lunch respite. I opened the bento and was startled at my discovery. There before me was a whole half of a roasted chicken with several mushroom-sauced rice balls and a lump of cooked mustard greens. On top was a pair of disposable chopsticks. I was overwhelmed at my good fortune.

I began tearing at the chicken with my fingers, chewing on large morsels accompanied by mouthfuls of rice balls and mustard greens. It was tasty and delectable. I found myself licking my fingers. When I finished I had a small problem of waste disposal. I threw the chicken bones into the woods knowing full well that some small animals or insects would feast on it. I then dug a hole in the soft earth to bury the cardboard box along with the paper napkins and spent chopsticks. I really enjoyed my meal and now thought about my next temple stop.

When I finished my disposal problem, I picked up my shoulder bag and continued walking with renewed energy having been fully sated. The road now seemed to veer in an easterly direction. I now felt certain that Temple 78, Gosho-ji was not too far off.

It was midday and I noticed an increase in automobile traffic going my way. After about an hour the road became much more improved until it eventually was made of hard gravel. I was aware of an increasing level of noise. Moreover, the traffic on the Takamatsu Expressway, which parallels my road, was becoming deafening. Far off, I could see the outline of the Ohashi railroad bridge going to Honshu. As I approached this intersection of the Takamatsu Expressway and the Ohashi Bridge, I had to make inquiries of local people as to the whereabouts of Temple 78, Gosho-ji. I finally received sufficient directions to lead me to the temple.

I was aghast at its appearance. It was an old wooden building with a wood shingle roof. There was moss growing at the eaves. At the front was a stone lantern, which seemed to be covered with soot. It was a depressing sight. I entered the hatto and found many pilgrims and some tourists engaged in ceaseless, heated conversation. This coupled with the highway din outside gave a welter of discordant sounds. I looked for the temple supervisor and spotted him in the center of the room. He appeared to be of middle age with a broad smile on his face as he spoke with the people, using many hand gestures. In approaching him I noticed several prominent stains on his black robe and a somewhat disheveled appearance. I asked to have my Fuda stamped, which he provided without comment. He seemed to be disconcerted as he hurried away. I performed my obeisance to the Buddha at the shrine and left in an urgent haste to get rid of the agitation of noise and turmoil. Breathing deeply outside, I decided to continue on to Temple 79, Tenno-ji.

XIV – TENNO-JI

It was quite an experience going from silent tranquility in the Na-katsu Barishoen Park to the raucous din of Temple 78. I later learned that Gosho-ji Temple is not Shingon but a different sect known as *Ji* with the deity as Amida. Could this be the reason for the confused state of affairs? But now I was on the road again walking away from the confusion and commotion.

I could see the sun dipping lower in the sky behind me and I hoped I would reach Temple 79 before dark. A long day's walk yet ahead of me with no plan; just a long ramble of hour after hour, entirely enjoyable. It ended at Temple 79, Tenno-ji. I arrived there at dusk, very tired; but in a joyful mood. I looked up to see the at-tenuated symmetry of the roof-line. This is a mark of a more na-tive Japanese taste. It was an unostentatious style in keeping with the tenets of the Shingon sect. I opened the door with a tremulous motion and went inside with a degree of expectancy. There was the temple supervisor sweeping the floor with a corn-broom. He looked up querulously. No one else was around.

"The temple is closed!"

"Oh, forgive me, honorable master. I have come a long way."

"Well then, come in and rest yourself."

"Thank you. I did not realize it was so late; otherwise I would have stopped at an Inn for the night."

"Have you eaten yet?"

"No, not since lunch."

"Well then, come and join me for some simple fair."

"I don't wish to intrude."

"Nonsense, you must eat to keep up your strength on your jour-ney."

"Thank you. I would enjoy accompanying you."

153

"Your payment will be to keep me company and have interesting conversation."

I followed him into the back room and sat at the table as he dished out the boiled rice with peas into two bowls. He handed one bowl to me with a pair of bamboo chopsticks and began eating. I was famished and started shoving the rice/peas combination into my mouth. It was very good but I was so hungry I didn't really have discretionary taste. We both had a second helping.

The temple supervisor ate with deft motions of his chopsticks, which I admired due to my own clumsiness. He was a small man about five feet six inches with a small hairless, tawny face, a pug nose and thick lips. He had a shaved head revealing a smooth round dome. On his neck was a large black mole, which drew my vision. He looked at me with piercing brown eyes with a multitude of laugh lines at the corners. I thought he must be about fifty years old. We both sat back as we sipped our tea.

He began picking his teeth with a bright metal pick while covering his mouth with his free hand while he labored. At the conclusion of teeth picking he put the metal pick in a small pouch and deposited it into his pocket.

"Tell me, dear sir, how old are you?"

I replied with some apprehension, "I am sixty-six years old."

He stared at me with open eyes, "Remarkable. You don't look that old and you seem very vigorous. Are you American?"

"Yes, I'm American"

"Have you studied Buddhism?"

"Well, I've read many Buddhist books and have practiced at the Minnesota Zen Center in America."

"I am curious why you are doing the Henro pilgrimage. Forgive me if I pry too much."

I had no choice but to repeat the usual litany, "Certain concepts of Buddhism have adroitly eluded me and I am trying to live a life of an ascetic in order to find the Buddhist ethic. I am particularly troubled by the concept of no self."

He began to speak in a didactic manner, "The phenomena of the material universe are, to Buddhists, unreal, since they exist only relative to each other and limited by time. Attachment to things therefore is evil and the source of all suffering. Buddhist practices aim at freeing men from earthly desires and preparing them by intellectual, psychological, or mystic means for "loss of self", that is, absorption into the undifferentiated real universe, independent of time and space. This loss of self is known as nirvana or "extinction" and is the Buddhist salvation."

"But is that the Buddhist ethic?"

Despite my interruption, he continued, "Buddhist ethics demand as the first human obligation sympathy for all beings. This sympathy should not be reserved solely for other men or even for all other sentient beings but belongs properly to the entire universe, inanimate as well as animate."

"I see."

"You look very tired. May I suggest that you stay the night? You can sleep in the temple. I can provide you with a blanket. And you can make a bed out of three zabutons (meditation mats) with a zafu (meditation cushion) as a pillow."

"You are too kind," I said.

"Come let me show you the bathroom where you can wash up."

He left as I took care of my toilet. When he returned he was wearing the most spellbinding kimono. I derived its beauty from intricate imagery set against deep azure settings.

"Your kimono is beautiful."

"Yes, I made it myself by a special traditional Japanese technique known as *katazome*. It utilizes a rice paste resist applied to fabric through stencils cut out of special paper. Then I can get a wide range of rich blues through indigo dying. You might say it is my hobby."

"I thought most Buddhist monks and priests practice calligraphy and haiku poetry."

"That is true. But I enjoy developing design ideas by observing and drawing from objects in nature, such as leaves, flowers, stones, and tree branches."

He was carrying the blanket, zafu and zabutons as we entered the hatto.

"I shall wake you at 4:30 am for morning meditation. Then we will have breakfast and you can be on your way. Good night."

"Thank you very much for all your kindness."

"Sleep well, my friend."

I placed the three zabutons in a row, removed my clothing and wrapped myself in the blanket. I fell asleep immediately. I must have been extremely tired after the long day. At 4:30 am the temple bell rang indicating it was time to get up. I put on my jacket as a substitute for a meditation robe (*kesa*) and went to the shrine with a zafu and zabuton. The temple supervisor was already sitting in meditation position. I placed my zafu and zabuton in parataxis at his side and began the art of zazen as I learned it in the Minnesota Zen Center. After forty minutes of sitting I heard a quiet tinkle of the meditation bell indicating the completion of meditation. By this time the incense stick I placed in the censor burned down.

The temple supervisor began chanting in a rhythmic, monotonous voice in Japanese with a low timbre overtone. I was fascinated by the sound and could only listen in uttermost amazement. When he completed the chant, he turned to me and grinning with drawn back lips, showing his teeth, began talking.

"Did you sleep well, my friend?"

"Yes, very well, indeed."

"I know Americans like to take showers. Would you like to take a shower?"

"Yes, I would, very much."

"Come with me and I will show you the bathroom. Incidentally, we have a western toilet."

After I finished with the bathroom necessities, including washing my walking stick, I dressed and met the temple supervisor in the small kitchenette that we occupied for dinner last night.

"This morning we have rice porridge known as congee for breakfast with some pickled daikon (white turnip). I hope you enjoy it."

"I really like congee and of course I have eaten many varieties of pickled vegetables in Japan. I consider them a culinary delight."

I sat down as he spooned out the thick porridge into what appeared to be the same bowls as last night. There was a plate of the pickled daikon in the center of the table. I began eating with the bamboo chopsticks helping myself to a morsel of pickled daikon every once in a while.

"How do you like it?"

With a mouthful, I said, "I am really enjoying myself."

He laughed as he said, "Come let us have tea. So, where will your next stop be?"

"I am heading for Temple 81, Shiromine-ji, then to Temple 82, Negoro-ji, and finally at the end of day four, I shall be at Temple 80, Kokubun-ji"

"Good. I see you know the shortest route. By the way, what is your name? My name is Yoshida."

"My name is Albert."

I thanked him profusely with a bow and a gassho as we parted.

"I hope you have a long and happy life, Reverend Yoshida."

"May you find what you are looking for, Mr. Albert?"

I left a 1000- yen bill in the donation box being very grateful for the kindness shown me. After saying goodbye, I walked out to meet the day and saw on the eastern horizon that the sun was beginning to appear. There were orange and yellow rays streaking across the dull gray sky. I picked up my shoulder bag and began walking with my walking stick out front.

XV – SHIROMINE-JI

Temple 81, Shiromine-ji is due north overlooking the Inland Sea. Temple 82, Negoro-ji is just east of that close to the coastline and Temple 80, Kokubun-ji is south back up to the hill area.

It is easy to see by looking on a map that most of the temples are grouped in clusters and most appear on the northern coastline. For example, Temples 67 to 87 are one group on the north and Temples 1 through 19 is another group situated on the east. Temples 28 to 36 are on the south coastline and Temples 44 to 53 are on the west as are Temples 54 to 64.This makes a total of 66 temples out of the total of 88.

There are literally hundreds of miles in between these group-ings dotted here and there with an isolated temple for the remaining 22. This obviously can make for burdensome and possibly feckless walking and probably is the reason most people ride in automobiles or buses. But, I contend that to do so prevent one from gaining the true flavor of Shikoku, which I really believe is what Kukai wanted. He saw this island as a Garden of Eden and wanted to share it with other people.

Walking along the road, in the dim light, I could hear the waves splashing up at the cliffside. I was heading for the pinnacle of the land while watching the sun rising at the east, to my right. On my left I could see the magnificent metal structure of the Ohashi Bridge, which connects the island of Shikoku with the mainland of Honshu. The gray metal of the bridge was reflecting the sunlight making it look silver. It reminded me of the Verrazano Bridge which spans the New York Harbor between Staten Island and Brooklyn in New York City. Then, I remembered that I was born and spent my youth only a few miles from there in Sheepshead Bay. I felt a tear in my eye as I reminisced about those halcyon days recalling a long forgotten time.

I began to miss my family. But I shook it off as I struggled uphill until I reached the lofty peak of the peninsula.

The view of the Inland Sea was strikingly beautiful and impressive. The sun was playing with the rippling water as it reflected tiny spots of light, which flashed with every merry movement. I could see many small boats plying in both directions while leaving a white wake in their trail. It was a magnificent sight and I silently vowed to sail those boats on the Inland Sea someday.

Turning right, along the jutting plateau, I followed the road until I arrived at Temple 81, Shiromine-ji in the early morning. It was a simple building with whitewashed stucco walled sides and a typical flowing, tiled roof. At the west end is a lovely moss garden that glows like a warm emerald in the filtered sunlight, giving a luminous and textured effect. There appeared to be several different kinds of moss in the garden. The entrance approach to the temple is visually rather striking since I had to go through a Japanese style arbor whose walls is set with plaques inscribed with poems.

I entered and found the hatto empty of people. I started to walk in to inspect the premises when the temple supervisor appeared out of the back room. He was an average size man wearing the usual black robes. He had the expected shaved head and his face appeared somewhat flaccid, which produced a double chin under a prominent lower jaw. He eyed me with severely slanted eyelids, which restricted my ability to see the color of his eyeballs. He smiled as he approached me with an upward curving of the corners of his mouth.

"Good morning, sir. How are you today? Please come in and welcome."

"Thank you. I was very impressed with your moss garden."

"Yes. It is very old. Moss is a very slow growing plant and the small animals burrowing for food often tear it up; but I care for it in my spare time. You are very early. Where are you coming from?"

"I just left Temple Tenno-ji where Reverend Yoshida put me up for the night."

"Yes. Reverend Yoshida is a very kind man."

Thinking I needed to confirm his statement I said, "Indeed, he is."

"It is very early and I don't expect any pilgrims or visitors until late morning. Would you care to join me for a cup of tea?"

"Yes. I would like that very much."

We walked together into the back room where a metal teapot was steaming on the stove. He rushed over to close the flame under the pot. I watched him spoon some crushed tea leaves into two earthenware mugs and hand one to me as I sat down. I found the small floating tea leaves getting caught in my mouth and on my teeth; it was unpleasant. I had no choice but to spit them back in the cup. Eventually the tealeaves settled to the bottom of the cup making it easier to enjoy the warm liquid. I should have exhibited some patience and allowed the tea cup to stand for a minute so the tealeaves could drop to the bottom. In a small way I felt ashamed for my coarseness.

He broke the ice by asking, "Tell me, kind sir, do you think there is a hidden force in nature that determines the way humans behaves?"

I felt it necessary to introduce myself, "My name is Albert Shansky."

"What. Oh I see, Shansky-san. My name is Nokubo."

"Now to answer your question, Reverend Nokubo; I am not sure if I know what you mean but I will try to explain my thoughts as best as I am able. There are writers known as vitalists such as Henri Bergson who nourish the Aristotelian belief that there is a driving intelligence behind nature and that natural processes are developed by this intelligence toward a desired end. This teleological, that is, goal-oriented system of belief easily becomes metaphysical if the intelligence is attributed to God or other supernatural force."

He hurriedly commented, "In Japan that is a basis for Shintoism. Shinto is a pantheistic religion, which believes that a god of sorts resides in all aspects of nature. Buddhists have tried to accommodate themselves to this teaching but I fear, it conflicts with the concept of self-reliance."

"Do you mean that you do not accept such a teaching?

"No. No. Buddhism doesn't say that a superior force in nature doesn't exist. It merely says that to attain salvation is up to the individual; waiting for external help is not the way."

"I see. Well it was very nice talking with you, Reverend Nokubo. I must be off to Temple Negoro-ji. Thank you very much for the tea."

"You are most welcome, Shansky-san. Have a good journey."

He stamped my Fuda while I made obeisance at the shrine. I left to go east to the next temple. Walking in the bright sun lifted my spirits and I plodded along looking across the placid Inland Sea, which appeared to be a giant lake. I spent a little time musing at this beautiful sight.

XVI – NEGORO-JI

Shortly before lunch I reached Temple 82, Negoro-ji. The day was pleasant; cool, easterly winds blew across the fields, and it was just warm enough with the sun starting up. I walked the landward edge of the fields, out of sight and sound of the sea. The plant life of the region is pushing through the surface drifts and green leaves of the beach-pea are thrusting up. When I strolled over to a thicket I found its buds tipped with a show of green.

Arriving at Temple 82, Negoro-ji, I saw the temple supervisor and his assistant airing the bedding and cleaning house. He hailed me from the back of the temple; we shouted pleasantries and passed the time of day.

"Good morning, Gaijin. Welcome, how are you this fine morning?"

"I am well, Reverend. How are you? Would you like my help?"

No, thank you. I am preparing for a large group that is coming from Takamatsu."

I queried, "A large group?"

"Yes, it is a tour group that started at Kyoto and is visiting many temples near the Takamatsu vicinity."

In looking up at the temple, I could see why it would be a tourist attraction. Some would find it garish, some beautiful and some interesting for its mixture of architectural styles. It looks more like an elegant, luxurious and extravagant villa than a temple with its groves, pond and gardens. The garden has some pleasant spots, the reflecting pond and the approaches are larger in scale than usual and the temple itself has some fine paintings and statues.

I entered the temple through the huge, iron-plated East Gate, richly ornamented with wood- carvings and metalwork. The inside is decorated with complex, and beautiful wood sculptures, murals, painted sliding doors, gilded and coffered ceilings and intricately carved soffits and transoms.

I went up to the shrine and found a large statue of the Buddha in back and an even larger statue of Kannon to its side. There was a large censor on the shrine, which contained spent incense stubs, which appeared like dead trees often seen drowning in a swamp. On each end of the shrine was an ornate brass candlestick bearing a lighted tall candle.

To one side of the middle of the table was a bowl containing a miniature statue of the Buddha sitting in water with a ladle with which to pour water over the Buddha for purification. I have often thought of this activity as a form of Baptism. Next to the water bath was a plate of mixed fruit, mostly apples and oranges.

I took three incense sticks, lit them and bowed three times before the Buddha. After placing them in the censor, I next went to the water bath and ladled some water over the small Buddha.

Having completed my obeisance, I turned around to look for the temple supervisor. I spotted him in the shadowy background. He had changed from his work clothes into the familiar black robes. As I walked up to him I could see that he was a taller than average man who's shaved dome had a stubble of hair beginning to grow back. He wore eyeglasses, which covered his eyes with thick bottle-glass lenses. His eyebrows were thick and black. His nose was sharply pointed and his mouth wore a perpetual smile or perhaps a grimace. When he spoke there was an upward movement of his lips, which made them appear stretched and thin.

"Reverend, could you please stamp my Fuda?"

"Ah, yes, dear sir. Give it to me, please."

I handed him the rolled up Fuda, which he took and stamped with the temple seal. He handed it back to me, rolled up, as if it were the most valuable document.

"Thank you, Reverend. When do you expect your guests from Takamatsu?"

"I am not sure but I would imagine in about an hour."

"Your temple is very beautiful."

"Thank you. It is about 600 years old. The original temple was devastated by fire so the local people rebuilt it with all the ornaments and accouterments that you see. The pond and garden were contributed by a delegation from Takamatsu about forty years ago as a gesture of peace after the Pacific War."

"I find that very interesting."

"Yes. This temple receives many guests both tourists and pilgrims."

"Well, I must be going now, Reverend. Thank you for the interesting talk."

"Go in peace, dear sir."

I left the temple to head for Temple 80, Kokubun-ji. The weather grew warmer toward late morning as the wind shifted to the south, ground mist swirled like a ghostly and sluggish sea around the rocks, shrubs, and windfall timber and it began to rain. I was thoroughly wet when the sun came out at noon but I began to dry quickly as I walked.

The country grew more open and rolling, more stony and barren with glacial rocks and the spruce forest thinned out. I needed the open, where the eye could see for miles. Sure enough, dead ahead I spotted several buildings. I hoped there might be a store among them in which to get something to eat. The wind changed in the afternoon and the sun warmed the earth as I approached the buildings lined up on both sides of the road.

I found a little bit of a place. A *Meiji* period coffee shop with what seemed to be authentic furnishings including a playing Pianola. As I entered I received a warm greeting from the proprietor and the clientele. I later learned that foreigners are always given an enthusiastic welcome. The place is basically a bar but they do serve other beverages as well as ice cream. I had to inquire about food.

I noticed some people at the bar eating bowls of soupy noodles. It looked very inviting so I ordered a bowl. When it arrived I saw that it contained noodles, tofu, wakame seaweed, shitake mushrooms, a whole egg and a fish cake. It was probably a version of *udon*. While eating I could hear the slurping sound made by the others who were drinking their soup by lifting the bowl to the lips.

XVII – KOKUBUN-JI

After a satisfactory lunch, I said goodbye to all and walked on to Temple 80, Kokubun-ji. On the way I passed a storefront in one of the buildings, which had small pictures of nature scenes hanging in the window. They were very striking, almost watercolor-like, which piqued my interest to the point that I was compelled to enter the store.

"Good day, I am interested in the pictures hanging in the window. Could you tell me about the technique?"

"Good day to you, sir. The technique is called *Moku Hanga* and is a type of Japanese woodblock printmaking. It enjoys the brilliance of watercolor using simple hand tools. Japanese woodblock technique differs radically from western relief-printing in that no press is used, no solvent other than water is needed, the pigment sinks deeply into the paper and colors may be repeatedly overprinted practically without limit. I had a solo exhibition of my prints in Kyoto last year; some of them are hanging in the window."

"I always thought of Ukiyo-e prints as being the premier Japanese woodblock print."

"Well that is true for the 17th and 18th centuries but there had begun a modification of the technique in the 19th and 20th centuries. Although Ukiyo-e is still being done, the new medium is now Maku Hanga, which depends on carving, registration, image transfer, and the use of the Baren, the traditional printing disk."

"But I am told people still collect Ukiyo-e woodblock prints and I understand some are very valuable."

"That is true. The reason they are so valuable is due to their history and culture. The Ukiyo-e or pictures of the floating world, which began to appear in the 17th century, are realistic representations of the actual world of the day. The idea that life is a floating world can be found in both East and West. For instance, it is stated in the Chinese classic *Chuang-tsu* that human life is adrift on the floating water called death, and Heraclitus, a Greek philosopher, said that all things were in a state of flux. This way of thinking became stronger in Japan than in China through the influence of Buddhism."

He continued, "The term Ukiyo originally was used in the Buddhist sense of the "transient and sad world". But when, after going through a period of incessant civil war, Japan became a society in which people could achieve success through ability, the term came to mean the "floating world" in which the fleeting pleasures of life were prized. In other words, the term came to be used in a worldly sense rather than in a religious one."

Without stopping he explained, "Ukiyo-e or floating world pictures at first referred only to pictures of everyday life at the time, but later came also to include those treating historical or fantastic subjects, whether they were painted on sheets of paper or mass-produced by means of wood-block printing. At any rate Ukiyo-e invariably represent the vital interests and concerns of the populace of the day, providing us with a good record of them."

"I see. I should like to buy one of your pictures. How much are they?"

"The ones in the window are 1000-yen each."

The proprietor rolled up the woodblock print and placed it in a cardboard tube. After handing it to me I paid him the 1000-yen. I placed the tube in my shoulder bag and bade him goodbye. I then left the store and continued my journey. After a while I could see the built-up area fading behind me. A few crows were moving about; one of them took a playful stoop at me and hit my head with its talons, knocking off my floppy hat. It then flew off with the familiar screeching *kak! Kak! Kak!* I waved at it with my walking stick; flying off it came to rest on a tree limb.

Within the hour a wind came up and gradually increased bringing a drop in temperature with it. The quiet and the drowsy, peaceful warmth were gone, and I took to plodding ahead again. Toward afternoon the wind died down bringing back the favorable weather.

As I walked along I passed several groups of pilgrims identifiable by their dress. I greeted all with a wave of my hand. Every so often a car with tourists would pass me as well. Arriving at Temple 80, Kokubun-ji I immediately recognized that it was built in modified Ming Chinese style. Inside there were richly textured gold screen paintings. The garden is full of variety, and the arrangements of the other support buildings allow it to be viewed from various angles. The entire complex is quite extensive and is relatively uncrowded with sightseers. Vegetarian food may be had at a restaurant just outside the gate anytime. Resting from my long walk found me sitting in the restaurant sipping tea.

Entering the temple I was greeted by the temple supervisor who bowed with a deep gassho.

"Welcome to Kokubun-ji."

"Thank you. The beauty of your temple impresses me."

"Yes. It is one of the most beautiful temples on the Henro route."

"Would you, please, stamp my Fuda?"

"Of course, I would be delighted to do so."

Following him I was able to leisurely savor the atmosphere and the life of the temple. It is a big, heavily timbered building with a wide overhanging tiled roof and black plastered walls resting on a high stone terrace. On the interior walls can be found beautiful paintings of birds in natural settings and there are a few notable sliding screen paintings.

After stamping and returning my Fuda I noticed that he was a rather middle-aged man with a dusky complexion and a massive buck-toothed smile.

"Are you American?"

"Yes, I'm American."

He looked at me with a slight grimace, "I notice from your Fuda that you started the Henro at Temple 68. That is unusual most people start at Temple One; but they rarely get beyond Temple 29, Kokubun-ji in Kochi, and our namesake."

"I suppose there are very few who complete the whole Henro on foot."

He laughed slightly, "That's true. Most that complete the Henro do so by automobile. There are others who do it in sections over a few years."

"Are all the Henro temples active? I mean do they all have regular services?"

"Many of the temples are active but they are usually the ones located near cities. The remote areas have temples, which are not active because they are difficult to reach on a regular basis."

"That's very interesting. Do you know of a small ryokan nearby where I can stay for the night?"

"Yes. There is a small ryokan just down the road about 50 meters."

"Thank you very much for your help."

"Go in peace, dear sir."

I stepped out into the late afternoon, which was mild and pleasant under a clear sky. Shadows lengthened across the road as I trudged down to the ryokan. There is no doubt I was tired walking up the path laboriously to the front entrance of the ryokan. I knocked on the door and was admitted with a low bow by the Okusan. I removed my shoes and entered the anteroom where I put on the provided house slippers.

"Good evening, Okusan. Do you have a room for me?"

"Welcome, dear sir. Yes there is a room for you but the bath is shared."

"That will be fine. Thank you."

She said in a very pleasant tone, "After you register, I shall show you to your room. You will have time to bathe before I bring your dinner."

I thanked her and followed her to my room. She insisted on carrying my shoulder bag; after a short, repeated pull and tug she snatched my bag. Despite my macho feeling I allowed her to carry it knowing it was not heavy. I undressed and put on the provided yukata. I had arranged to have my clothes washed and ironed overnight so I put them in the provided laundry bag.

I then went into the communal bathroom. To one side of the bathroom was an 8 ft. by 8 ft. white tiled tub, which contained hot water. Steam was rising from the surface making it look very inviting. Along the wall periphery of the room was about ten stations with hot and cold spigots, each about one foot off the floor. In front of each station was a small wooden bench on which one sits to soap up and scrub.

I completed my soaping and scrubbing and then rinsed off the lather with a wooden bucket of water, which I spilled several times over my head. I then entered the tub. It seemed like floating in a Bain-Marie; so warm and comforting giving a contented feeling of well being. I stretched out my legs to allow my leg muscles to ease. I remembered a slight irritation at my perineum, which seemed to soothe away by the warm water.

There were two other men in the tub who were laughing and talking loudly. I acknowledged them with a friendly greeting. I am sure they were laughing at my accent. After leaving the tub and briskly towel drying I returned to my room. It was then that I noticed its small size. It was about ten feet by twelve feet but free of furniture except for a small table at one corner containing a lamp and a Thermos (vacuum bottle) of hot water with a canister of ground tealeaves and a cup. The futon on which I was to sleep was rolled up in the small closet.

In about a half hour I could hear the Okusan fussing outside my sliding door. She opened the door and brought in a tray with my dinner. It contained a bowl of clear soup with two flower-shaped prawns. The prawns were cooked in salted *niban-dashi* (bonito soup stock). Shitake mushrooms and cooked asparagus were all swimming in a clear bonito soup. In addition, there was a plate of fried lotus root, grilled meat and vegetables and a large bowl of cooked rice *(gohan)*. After eating my dinner I placed the tray of dishes and my laundry bag outside my door in the hallway. I then removed the futon from the closet and fell asleep while creeping inside. Thus, ended the fourth day without fanfare.

XVIII – ICHINOMIYA-JI

I awoke at 5:00 am, showered, shaved and dressed in the clean clothes left outside my room. At 6:00 am the Okusan brought my breakfast, which consisted of a bowl of steaming cooked rice and a fried mackerel, with a plate of pickled lotus root. After breakfast I paid my bill and departed in search of Temple 83, Ichinomiya-ji. I headed down the road in a southeasterly direction. The road looked lonely; there were no people within my view; only a single house and a scattered group of ungulates. The wind had shifted to the south during the night, and there were multitudes of birds in the thickets.

The sun was getting higher now and the checkered farming country with its pinewoods abounded everywhere. Several migrating birds were in sight and half a mile away, perched on top of a pole, was what I thought to be an old, haggard hawk that paid no attention to me. Presently a lone Monarch butterfly fluttered past her. This incredible traveler, so small and fragile that it seemed at the mercy of the slightest breeze, would find its way and migrate as far as her course would take her. I watched it diminish and disappear across the level land.

The road went on and passed through an opening in the pines where the ruin of an old hotel stood. Most of the roof had fallen in. The porches had collapsed, and broken, weathered shingles from its walls littered the ground around it. Now it had a melancholy air of gaunt decay. I continued on but found my direction was suddenly turning directly east.

Walking into the intensity of the rising sun almost blinded my view. I walked this way for two hours until the direct sun abated. I grew tired; my muscles ached from walking against the wind but this had to be endured. I was spent and decided to sit on a boulder at the side of the road to rest. I realized my condition, accepted it, and made the best of it.

Feeling the sweet coolness of the early morning air I got up to continue my journey. A great joy went through me as I spotted the temple in the distance. With my eyes still on the far horizon I approached the temple area.

Many visitors to Japan are confused between a temple and a shrine. A temple is a Buddhist place of worship, and is devoted to purely religious functions. Most temples in Japan have the suffix *–ji* after the name meaning "temple". Shrines are associated with the Shinto religion, which is purely Japanese having its roots in primitive nature-worship. Most Shrines can be easily identified by the peculiar gateway called the *torii*, the basic form of which is two logs placed horizontally on the top of two pillars to form an archway. Suffixes such as *jinja and jingu* usually indicate a Shinto shrine. Shrines are centers of neighborhood activities and non-religious functions are held in the shrine precincts.

Arriving at the temple, I noticed that the priest of the temple was blessing an automobile. The car is surrounded by flowers, and the priest accompanied by two boy acolytes, drive the evil spirits away thus insuring that the car will never be involved in an accident. Devout believers arrive with freshly washed automobiles, willing to pay about 300-yen for the ceremony and receive a small amulet, the Buddhist equivalent of a St. Christopher's medal.

At the conclusion of the ceremony the car owner drove away feeling very satisfied. The temple building is not particularly distinguished for its beauty or any significant art. The most impressive feature of the temple is, perhaps, the large number of pilgrims in attendance. Some participate with an act of penance consisting of pouring ice- cold water over their bodies.

Walking inside the *hatto* I found the priest who performed the car purification and asked him to stamp my Fuda. Outside I found a rustic wooden bench about sixty inches long called a Samurai seat made of hewn cedar logs. It had Japanese characters written into the edging, which I could not translate. I sat down to rest. In a few minutes a middle- age gentleman sat next to me. He was dressed in the Henro costume. As he sat down he removed his hat. Most of his hair was gone and there were brown age-spots dotting his dome. The patches around his ears are thin and mostly gray. He wears wire-rimmed glasses that are quite thick and somewhat dirty. His fore-head is divided into two round halves that meet pretty much in the center, where a deep crease joins them then plummets to his nose. He is one of the most unattractive men I've ever seen. His skin color is tawny but his face bears the ravages of smallpox. When he talks his nose wrinkles and his upper lip rises to reveal four large upper teeth. He appears to be about fifty years old. His dress is shabby and the collar of his stained white jacket is frayed. Sitting without offering a gassho or a handshake or a smile he opens the conversation.

"My name is Shoka Watanabe. Are you on the Henro pilgrimage?"

"Yes, I am."

"Where are you from?"

"I am American."

"Ah! American, welcome to Japan."

"Thank you."

"What is your name?"

"My name is Albert Shansky."

"Do you enjoy Japanese art?"

"Yes, I do, very much."

He puffed out his chest and said, "Ikebana (flower arranging) is one of the arts, which I have cultivated as a hobby. Some years ago I attended an Ikebana class at the Sogetsu School in Tokyo; Ever since I have been practicing in my spare time.

"Would you please explain Ikebana to me? I know nothing about it."

He began to speak in a teaching-like manner, "Ikebana is the practice of flower contemplation. It is known as *kado*, the way of flowers. By the 15ᵗʰ century, informal traditions of floral arranging became formalized into distinct, stylistic "schools" – each with their own oral and written teachings, and each with their own line of master teachers. These exist today as the Ohara, Ikenobo, and Sogetsu schools. Seen in terms of religion, the art of flower-arranging has been influenced by all the religions of Japan and has become, in its own right, an important part of a Japanese religio-aesthetic tradition, in which artistic disciplines and creativity carry important religious meaning as "ways" of spiritual fulfillment. This can be compared to the Chinese Taoist *Tao* or the way."

I was overwhelmed by his explanation, "I see. In my limited experience I always think of Ikebana as equivalent to the tea ceremony; nothing more than an aesthetic pursuit."

He threw his head back and said, "No, indeed, Shansky-san. Both of those endeavors have religious overtones. In the Sogetsu School we are taught to arrange the flower according to the movements of the body and its extremities much like a T'ai Chi Chuan pose."

Though you see the back of another you cannot see your own

"What do you do with the finished arrangement?"

"Sometimes I place the exceptional ones in the *tokonoma* (alcove) at home. Other times I just take a photograph, which I include in an album. I have hundreds of photos."

"That's very interesting. What about Bonsai?"

"Bonsai is truly aesthetic without religious implications. It is a way of producing and cultivating miniature plants and sometimes miniature landscapes. Although it can be considered an art form or a craft it has no religious significance other than imitating nature in miniature."

"Bonsai is very popular in America. One can buy finished items in garden shops along with kits for making your own."

He said, with some pride, "In Japan there are contests, which are graded by experts who dispense awards to winners. There are also exhibits and permanent collections."

"Thank you for the interesting conversation."

"How long have you been on the Henro?"

"This is my fifth day and I am now heading north to Temple 84, Yashima-ji. Goodbye and thank you once again."

XIX – YASHIMA-JI

I left him sitting on the bench. With a wave of my hand I headed down the road. My destination was the Yashima peninsula overlooking the Inland Sea. I intend following the Kotoden Kotohira Railroad Line and bypass the city of Takamatsu until I reached the Yashima peninsula.

I descended a steep hill, and approached the hemlocks through a large sugar bush. As I enter the woods a black-colored crow starts up before me and caws sharply. His protest when thus disturbed is almost metallic in its sharpness.

Passing down through the maple arches, barely pausing to observe the antics of a trio of squirrels, - two gray ones and a black one, - I cross an ancient brush fence and am fairly within the old hemlocks, and in one of the most primitive, undisturbed nooks.

In the deep moss I tread as with muffled feet, and the pupils of my eyes dilate in the dim almost religious light. After leaving the woods I walk along the old road, which now begins to parallel the railroad tracks seen in the distance. I note animal tracks in the thin layer of mud. When do these creatures travel here?

I have never yet chanced to meet one. There is as much wildness in the track of an animal as in its voice. Everywhere in these solitudes I am greeted with the pensive almost pathetic presence of the indigenous animals. Coming to a drier and less mossy place along the road I continued walking with renewed vigor. Turning to the left from the old road, I wander over soft logs and gray yielding debris, across a little brook, until I emerge in the overgrown trees with peeling bark.

In a little opening quite free from brush and trees, I step down to bathe my hands in the brook, when a small, light slate-colored bird flutters out of the bank, not three feet from my head, as I stoop down, and as if severely lamed or injured, flutters through the grass and into the nearest bush.

I pause now and then on my way to admire a small, solitary white flower, which rises above the moss, with radical heart shaped leaves. It is completely unknown to me. Looking away, I observe the ferns, of which I count six varieties. I then find myself in close proximity to the railroad tracks and turn right to follow them north towards my destination.

After two hours of steady walking, I began to come upon a more civilized area with houses and people. I try to avoid and circumvent these places by staying close to the shoreline along the peninsula. Walking along this shore road there remains a clump of cedars, and the dead post oaks are ranged in rows, and branches that belong to trees of the same kind may be pulled out of the peat that in places forms little cliffs. This peat was originally formed when the present shore was part of a salt meadow.

Cedar trees may also be seen dead or dying, the trunks buried a foot or more in the sand, or the soil washed away from their roots, which sprawl in a ghastly fashion mid dead crabs and the wrecks of things that the Inland Sea has thrown away. What a marvelous hoard of dead creatures the sea casts up to the land.

The gulls rejoice at the death of the crab and they frequent in numbers the sandy points, from which they rise with weird screams. They often sit motionless in rows at low tide, apparently many of them asleep, and when the tide rises they float on the waves in nearly the same place where they were standing before. I walked inland for a short distance and finally came upon Temple 84, Yashima-ji.

I am now standing on the Yashima Tableland, once called the "Roof of the Inland Sea," the site of Yashima Temple that looks down on Takamatsu City five miles away. It was at the foot of this headland that a bloody and decisive sea battle was fought between the rival Genji and Heike clans in 1184. A museum in the temple is filled with relics of the battle, in which the Heike warriors were overwhelmingly defeated. A view from the Yashima Tableland is

Futago Bay, which is famous for clam hunting. Legend has it that the crabs found at the foot of this headland with their back markings that look like a human face, are the ghosts of the armor-clad warriors who drowned during the battle.

Ahead are olive groves, transplanted from Europe, granite cliffs and, of course, some of the 88 temples of the Henro.

Outside of the temple grounds was a street vendor selling bowls of a native dish called the Once Upon a Time Genji and Heike Stew (*Mukashi-gatari Gempei-nabe)*. It contains meat of a pigeon, chopped crabs, fish paste and curly Chinese cabbage with fried, dried wheat. It was delicious and filling and I enjoyed it very much.

The Yashima Temple lies somewhat hidden in a grove of cryptomeria trees. It is a beautiful example of early Buddhist architecture and an amazing demonstration of what Japanese builders could do with wood. The two great pillars that support the edifice are over 50 feet high. The combination of grace and strength too is unique, and Japanese. Gleaming white walls topped by a black tiled roof trimmed in white mortar, soaring lines that bristle with horned corners and sculptured detail truly make this one of the most beautiful temples on the Henro. The extensive outworks are like a park, full of walls, gates, ponds and living quarters. This is a carefully preserved, wholly authentic example of a temple unique in the world, for it is a work of art as well.

On entering the temple I was greeted by a loud din from the crowds of tourists and pilgrims in the Hatto. They were attracting considerable attention to themselves with their jabbering, laughing, and fatuously enjoying their own exaggerated gestures. I noticed the temple supervisor – he was old – no doubt about it – for wrinkles surrounded his eyes and mouth. There was a dull flush on his cheeks; his head was freshly shaven, his neck a gnarl of sinews and a toothy yellow grin whenever he laughed. Unnerved, I watched him moving in the company of these tourists until I was able to approach him. I asked to have my Fuda stamped and then performed obeisance at the shrine before I left. I sensed myself gliding away from the crowd and the confusion of the voices.

I felt as though not everything was getting off to exactly its usual start, as though a dreamlike strangeness were beginning to expand and engulf the world, a bizarre metamorphosis to which a stop might be put if I could briefly shade my eyes, and then take another look around. I continued on my way walking in the direction of the second peninsula *Aji* to Temple 85, Yakuri-ji.

I hadn't even considered the possibility of it being otherwise, since the day had always greeted me in full splendor. But now, the sky and sea remained gloomy and leaden, misty rain fell intermittently and I found myself approaching a different land at peninsula *Aji* than I encountered just an hour before. There to my right, the flat coastline began to emerge, fishing boats dotted the Inland Sea, and little islands began to appear.

Bleary-eyed, my staff trembling between my fingers, I swayed as I stood at the coastline edge, struggling to maintain my balance. I dared not take a step for fear of falling down. Feeling the warm breath of a sirocco, I stepped back and continued down the path to the road. I closed my eyes to savor a moment of self-indulgence, as unfamiliar as it was sweet.

It was growing quiet around me. Nothing could be heard except the dull slap of the waves against the rocky shore – and a second sound as well, a murmuring, a muttering; the hissing of the wind through the trees. A broad horizon spread before me, tolerantly encompassing great diversity.

Every mood of the wind, every change in the day's weather, every phase of the tide – all these have subtle sea music's all their own. The dominant note is the great spilling crash made by each arriving wave. It may be hollow and booming, it may be heavy and churning, it may be a tumbling roar. The second fundamental sound is the wild seething cataract roar of the wave's dissolution and the rush of its foaming waters up the beach.

XX – YAKURI-JI

As I came to Temple Yakuri-ji, the sun broke through and the gloomy clouds disappeared. Temple Yakuri-ji is one of the largest temples in Shikoku, but is not particularly distinguished for its beauty or any significant art. The most impressive feature of the temple is, perhaps, the large number of pilgrims constantly in attendance. Many stay several days to enjoy the proximity of the sea and beaches. A seashore road will take them to the beach, now fast being converted into a mass leisure-recreation complex. A pleasant drive will bring the traveler back across the neck of the peninsula through lovely antiquated villages.

I made arrangements to stay at the temple overnight. After I was provided with a futon in a separate building in a dormitory style setting I went about the business of locating a restaurant in which to eat dinner. While walking down to the beach I came to a restaurant right on the beach called Gahama, which served tempura and other fish courses together with the ubiquitous cooked rice (gohan). It was moderately priced with excellent and friendly service.

The local farmers told me that there would be a performance of a puppet show this evening in an outdoor setting. This would be the traditional art of folk puppetry. The hand puppet show retains an old style popular before *Bunraku* (puppetry). It flourished in the days when entertainment was rare in rural villages. One man, who uses his right hand for manipulating the puppet's head and arms, and his left hand for moving the strings controlling the eyelids and mouth, operates each puppet. The villagers adapted the performance style to their own taste by incorporating local dialect and erotic jokes. It has fortunately been preserved in this area although folk puppetry is dying out in favor of the more classical *Bunraku* found in the cities.

After the performance I returned to the temple dormitory to sleep in my futon. Thus, day five ended.

The night noises in the dormitory prevented me from getting an adequate sleep. Some people were snoring; others were talking in whispers. After tossing and turning, I finally fell asleep. Rising very early in the morning of day six while it was still dark, I dressed to pursue Temple 86. Temple 86, Shido-ji is near the city of Shido due south at the end of the peninsula Aji. Once again, I followed the local road, which hugged the coastline of Aji until I reached the outskirts of the town of Shido, whose silhouetted roofs I could dimly glimpse in the distance. Just before the town, I found a local restaurant, which surprisingly was open that time of day. I had a bowl of miso soup and a plate of soba noodles for breakfast.

XXI – SHODO-JI

Afterwards I began walking with long strides, shivering slightly in my thin chinos and cotton jacket. I was rather hampered by the shoulder bag, which I wedged against my ribs, first under one arm, then under the other, so that I could keep both hands plunged deep in my pockets in order to avoid the whiplash of the wind. I had only one thought in my head; the hope that the cold wind would be less after daybreak

There was a sign of dawn ready to relight the dead sky, as I walked along. Amid the fields of rice and lentils the village slumbered in the depths of night. You could just detect the back to back houses, running geometrically in parallel lines like a barracks, and divided by three wide avenues, laid out with regular gardens. And, over the deserted plain, the only sound to be heard was the wailing of the wind, tearing the trellises away from the fences. The town clock struck five o'clock echoing with five chimes, but nothing stirred.

As I walked along the wide avenue I came upon a thin, gangling young man, whose long face was darkened at the chin, shadowed by a few scraps of nascent beard. He had brown-colored hair and an anemic complexion. His shirt had ridden up around his belly, and he tugged it down again, not from modesty, but to keep himself warm.

"Excuse me, would you please tell me the way to Temple Shi-do?"

He gave a good-natured laugh. He was so small, with thin limbs, and his fierce brown eyes lighted up his livid monkey-like features. His tight, curly hair and his big ears emphasized the pallor of his sullen, angry features, and, he said:

"Walk straight ahead to the next intersection and then turn right on the road out of town for about two kilometers."

"Thank you for your help."

"I think the temple is closed now."

"Thank you. I'll wait there until it opens."

The wind was still strong, but the light playing on the low walls of the village buildings were brighter now, and the air was filled with muffled sounds of people waking up. Already doors were opening and closing, as dark lines of people moved off into the night.

"Hello there, said a man who was closing the door of a neighboring house."

"Hello!" I returned.

"Where are you off?"

"I am going to Temple Shido."

"Oh, yes, straight ahead. It opens at six o'clock."

"Thank you."

Back in the village the lights started to go on and the doors banged shut. All the way from the silent village I walked until I reached Temple Shido, wending my way through the gusts of wind.

When I reached the temple I had to mount a dark stone staircase, and found myself on a gangway leading across a flowing, gurgling brook, which was so plunged in darkness that I groped my way forward with outstretched arms to avoid bumping into things. I opened the temple door. Suddenly two large yellow eyes cut through the darkness. He was a fat man with a face like a benevolent policeman, and a wide gray moustache.

"Good morning, dear sir."

"Good morning, Reverend. Is the temple open?"

"Yes, come in. I am just unlatching the door. Are you on the Henro Pilgrimage?"

"Yes, I am. I hope I am not disturbing you so early."

"Not at all, our day begins at six o'clock after meditation."

The vast hall seemed like the nave of a church, haunted by great, floundering souls. The only bright patch came from the lamp blazing at the end of the room. For a moment I stood motionless, blinded. I felt frozen until I got used to my surroundings, and my eyes became accustomed to the darkness.

"Would you, please, stamp my Fuda, Reverend?"

"Of course I shall, dear sir."

"Thank you. How far is Temple 88, Okuboji from here?"

"Oh, it's about fifteen kilometers, but all up hill. Okuboji is in the mountains."

"Thank you. I'd better get started. I'm on my way to Temple 87, Nagao-ji, first."

"May your road be blessed?"

I took the Fuda, which the temple supervisor returned to me. I then went to the shrine to make my obeisance. When I turned he was nowhere to be seen. I left the temple with the earthen aroma of stone architecture, into the bright sunshine, heading south. The wind had died down and it looked to be a salubrious day.

If a fool looks into the mirror a sage will not look out.

XXII – NAGAO-JI

All the way along the road automobiles and trucks passed me. Some drivers waved at me and I returned their greetings. Shortly before noon I reached the town of Nagao where Temple Nagao-ji was located. It was a difficult uphill walk but the weather was calm and warm.

As I approached Temple Nagao I was struck by the singing of cicadas in the foundation of rocks. Throngs of pilgrims who were made obvious by their white garb occupied the temple grounds. They walked about insouciantly inspecting and observing the temple buildings. There was a large gate separating the temple grounds from the road. To the right of the temple plaza was a dining hall in front of which was a Samurai bench. Straight ahead was the main temple in which was located the *hatto*. The architecture of the temple was unique in that it had what looked like a double roof shaped like a two-tier pagoda. I took care of my Fuda stamping and did my obeisance and then departed for the long trek to Temple Obuko-ji.

As I got out on the road the sun was almost directly overhead and beating down on me mercilessly. After a few minutes a tractor came along side of me and the driver began to shout at me.

"Gaijin (foreigner) do you want a ride?"

I looked at him long and pensively. He was a farmer wearing a straw hat and the usual style Japanese gray work clothes with balloon pants and leggings. His clothes were all dirty and dusty. His face was relatively smooth except for day old stubble. His skin was very dark and tawny and he showed large buckteeth when he smiled. His eyes were narrow slits.

I hesitated and wondered what to do for a moment but then became quickly convinced when I heard the sound of rainfall. I then climbed up into the cage of the tractor. At first a few large drops had rung out on the roof of the cage, like the start of a downpour, and now the rain increased, streaming down as it turned into a veritable deluge. The roof of the cage must have been leaking, for a trickle of water ran down my shoulder and soaked through to my skin. The farmer said:

"Good thing you climbed aboard, Gaijin. Where are you going?"

"I am going to Temple Okuboji."

"What luck, I am heading there too. I have several small rice paddies in that area which I am going to till today."

"May I join you all the way?"

Of course, I would delight in your company."

"Do you know of a place I can stay for the night?"

"Yes, indeed. You should go to see Mrs. Uchida in Okubo town. She has a cabin, which she sometimes rents to travelers. Tell her Gomba sent you."

"Is that your name, Gomba?"

"Yes. What is your name?"

"My name is Shansky."

"I am very happy to know you Shansky-kun (Mr. Shansky)."

We shook hands in the western manner and continued our journey with question and answer conversation until we reached Temple 88, Okubo-ji. We parted with fond goodbyes as the rain stopped and the sun returned once again.

XXIII – OKUBO-JI

Okubo-ji is the twentieth temple I have visited in six days. The temple was a very large edifice with many pilgrims and tourists in the foreground of the temple. Some people were sitting on the grass in groups talking aimlessly. As a skeptical visitor, I can describe the reverential atmosphere and the behavior it engendered, observing people discussing under old trees the deepest problems of life, and greeting one another with smiles of forgiveness and looks of understanding. They seemed incapable of saying any but the holiest of things. They look deep into your eyes when they talk to you.

The tourists have a weakness for sandals, with clothes without any particular distinction of shape, for the rougher kind of textiles. The pilgrims all wear similar white uniforms almost a breed apart. The men affect long hair, while the women keep theirs short. They do their best to copy the leader, to be kind and sincere or to make jokes and show how jolly they are. These were all symptomatic of egos that desired massage rather than dissolution. Not a bid for transformation but the replacement of one set of social conditions for another.

I hurriedly took care of my needs inside the temple and had my Fuda stamped. I bade goodbye to the temple supervisor who seemed dismayed at my hasty departure. I explained that I wanted to reach Mrs. Uchida's cabin before dark. I hoped he understood. I then went in search of Mrs. Uchida and her cabin.

At a little after midday I reached the town of Okubo, the home of the 88th temple on the Henro route, where I hoped I could wash and eat a hearty meal; perhaps of fish and rice and drink Japanese green tea.

I continued walking along meadows lush with grass and herbs and bordered by a lively stream. Beyond, ahead rising into a bluer and bluer sky was a limestone and granite outcropping. While walking I was rewarded by a glimpse, through the stands of pine trees and black firs, of a feral animal or an agreeably equalizing roadside exchange of greetings, *konnichiwa* (good day) with a peasant wearing a long white cloak and the distinctive male head gear, a black felt hat, which he doffed at the welcome sight of the foreign stranger from the big city.

It would be another three hours before I reached the upper valley, some five hundred meters high, where the village nested. With luck it would be just sunset when I came into the village to take up a borrowed peasant life, having been told, by the farmer Gomba that I could rent a cabin from an old widow, Mrs. Uchida, for a few days.

I occupied a low square hut with two rooms, one that could be used as a sleeping chamber. Like every dwelling in the village, this hut was an ingenious sculpture of spruce logs (the region abounded in spruce forests) with joints dovetailed at the end, while its few heavy chairs, tables, and slatted bed were carpentered from the more expensive, pinkish larch.

Within minutes of my arrival I had flung open the dull-paned windows to air out the garlic reek. I distributed in a cupboard and on wall peg my minimum possessions – bringing so little was also part of the adventure – and was ready to start enjoying my unencumbered freedom. I looked forward to walking barefoot in the grass and bathing in the icy stream at dawn.

I swept and chopped wood and collected the water for bathing and laundry. Only the cooking was left to the huts owner, Mrs. Uchida, an elderly widow who moved in with her sister's family during my stay. The day was organized around her ample meals of breakfast and dinner.

For dinner, Mrs. Uchida brought me *katsu don,* which are deep fried, bread-crumbed pork cutlet, onions and softly scrambled egg covered in sauce on boiled rice. There were two side dishes of *kappa-maki* (pickled cucumber) and *takuan-maki* (pickled white radish).

After dinner I decide to walk among the moonlit trees. The wind had risen, and the silent forest seemed to thrum and whisper. Then my moment of rapt attention disclosed, to my dismay, to my fear, a sinister rustling noise. It could be, I reminded myself, the sound of ripe acorns breaking loose from their pedicels and rustling through the leaves as they fell to the ground. It could also be the stealthy approach of a bear, about to jump from behind the tree and tear open my throat before I could utter a cry.

Lashed by fear, all my senses brought me fresh news. I could even detect, among the forest fragrances, a far off stench of skunk. And the noises – hooting owls and another fainter rustling sound; and then ... blessed silence, which I greeted with choking relief and gratitude, as if I had received a reassuring message from nature itself. All was well all would be well. It was not that I entertained any fantasy of being invulnerable; I was too rational for that. But nothing could route my immense feeling of well being and self-approval. Even if my life ended now, I said to myself, my God, what a journey I have made. I certainly am not a thanatophobe; I have no fear of death.

I entered the cabin and prepared for bed. My bed moving across the floor awakened me during the night. A "small" earthquake, according to the villagers, and apparently common in the islands of Japan, though it is the first I have felt on this trip. I remained in the hut for three days luxuriating in solitude that I enjoyed thoroughly. But, I now had to think about getting to Tokyo for a previously scheduled business meeting, which I just remembered making. First, I must reach my goods safely harbored in the Ryokan Shintokiwa in Takamatsu.

The next morning, after the third day in the cabin at Okubo, I decided to leave in order to get to the appointment on time. I felt so stupid at having forgotten about this commitment when I arranged to go on the Henro Pilgrimage. After a breakfast of congee sprinkled with ground sesame seeds and a pot of green tea, I said goodbye to Mrs. Uchida who responded with a toothless smile and headed for

National Road 183 to try my luck at hitchhiking to Takamatsu. After about one hour of walking and waiting a traveler who left me off at the outskirts of Takamatsu city picked me up.

While walking to the center of town things began to seem familiar to me. Eventually I came upon Ryokan Shintokiwa and as I entered I greeted the proprietor:

"Good morning!"

"Good morning, Gaijin. You are back sooner than expected."

"Yes. I have to go to Tokyo on business so I could not complete the Henro."

"Well you have only been gone a little more than a week. I thought you might be away as much as a month."

"I know it is somewhat confusing but you see I completely forgot about my appointment in Tokyo when I started out until yesterday when I realized, while staying in a cabin in Okubo, that it was most important for me to attend this meeting."

"Of course, these things happen. How did you like the Henro?"

"It was quite an experience and I thoroughly enjoyed my travels. Shikoku is a truly beautiful island. Maybe someday I'll return to finish the whole Henro route."

"I hope so. Let me get your left luggage."

"Thank you for all your help and give my regards to the Okusan."

"Goodbye, Gaijin. Have a good life."

After I left I realized that these people are very provincial and somewhat xenophobic. Leaving the Ryokan, I walked to the pier to board the boat to Osaka. While on board as we "sailed" across the Inland Sea my thoughts went back to my time and adventures in Shikoku.

Shikoku is rich in historical and cultural heritage, which its people handed down from generation to generation since the ancient days to the present day. Now people visit historical relics to trace the footsteps of their ancestors, worship at shrines and temples to feel their pious hearts, and stand at castle remains to remember their rise and fall. People will sense the immeasurable implications the history and culture have on their life and feel awed by the gravity of the role they must play in handing down the precious heritage as well as their new cultural inventions to future generations.

For me the Divine Walk seemed to take a lifetime rather than the mere week I spent in going from temple to temple under somewhat arduous conditions. Perhaps it had to do with the quality and state of being a real event. I am suggesting that subconsciously reality has no predictable pattern, but is arbitrary and insubstantial. There is within this worldview a terrifying personal implication: that I myself have no fixed identity but am, like the rest of reality, essentially fluid – essentially inessential.

After the boat landed and I debarked, I had to walk about a half mile to the elevated train, which took me to Shin-Osaka where I caught the "bullet" train to Tokyo. I stayed overnight in Tokyo and in the morning I took the train to Yokohama where a prearranged automobile was waiting to take me to the Shiseido Research Center.

At the research center I met with my client-contact Tatsuya Ozawa. We greeted each other with a handshake and much backslapping. I was introduced to the other staff members in the reception room where we all sat for the inevitable cup of tea and small talk. Tatsuya Ozawa began with a friendly question.

"Well, Albert, tell me about your adventures in Shikoku. Did you go on the Henro pilgrimage?"

"I only did about a fourth of it. I did not have enough time to do anymore."

"Even that is more than most people do. I assume you walked the route rather than by car or bus."

"Yes. I started at Temple 68 and left after Temple 88."

"How long were you gone?"

"Only six days."

"Tell me, Albert, why did you go on the Henro?"

I looked at Tatsuya Ozawa for a long time before answering. I was gathering my thoughts and then began speaking slowly.

"I set out to find the Buddhist ethic by putting myself in tough situations: trekking exhaustingly high into mountainous areas, suffering the impact of icy rain storms, and sleeping on the floor of a cold temple. By exploring the connections between struggle and growth, fear and transcendence, and doubt and faith – I hoped to follow the great historical figures of Buddhism who encountered revelation in moments of great anguish. I did this while confronting my lifelong questions about spirituality, mortality, and my own self-worth. This *ethos* proved to be an authentic quest for an authentic spirituality. But more importantly it became an endeavor of an ultimate struggle – not so much with fate and death as with me. Along the way I found it to be a deep exploration of ordinary day-to-day living and its ultimate meaning which extends far beyond suffering and unimaginable isolation."

"Thank you for the explanation. I know I could never do such labor. But I see it has much meaning for you."

With that we adjourned to another room to carry on our business.

In the words of T.S.Eliot, "In the end is my beginning."

AFTERWORD

No amount of ingenuity can make much more of this story than what I myself say it is: a private handle on these places and characters that provided me with knowledge and amusement. The story is based on an actual event. In 1991 the author attempted the Henro Pilgrimage by walking from Takamatsu to Kochi, about 300 miles in two weeks, visiting about 42 temples.

At that time I was a guest at the Hosshinji Monastery in Obama, Japan for one week. I went there at the suggestion of Katagiri Roshi, the Abbot of the Minnesota Zen Center. During my stay in Hosshinji I befriended the monk, Taizan Shaeffer who told me about the Henro Pilgrimage. I then decided to attempt at least part of it. I walked about 300 miles from Takamatsu to Kochi in two weeks then took the train at Kochi and returned to Takamatsu where I boarded a boat to Osaka and thence a train to Tokyo; In order to make a business appointment at the Shiseido Research Center in Yokohama.

Actually this account of my Henro adventure logically and temporally precedes my Buddhist activities in the Hosshinji Monastery during the years 1992, 1993, and 1994 as well as the six following years as Executive Vice President of the International Institute for Field-Being.

I am a chemist who has dabbled in philosophy. I have written over sixty scientific papers and about twelve papers on philosophy. While I understand the connections between science and art as well as anyone, I am also well aware of the distinctions between writing a novel and drafting an article for some academic journal.

I readily admit that my own pronouncements on the matter of the Henro are enigmatic rather than clarifying. I use the Henro as a device for revealing the Buddhist ethic.

The architecture, art, museums, and temples discussed in this story are real in every sense of the word. Moreover, the descriptions of the temple supervisors are meant to depict the ordinariness of Buddhist monks and priests. In doing so I did not mean to besmirch anyone. None of the characters in this story are composites of people. I have met all of them in my many travels to Japan. If I have offended anyone I ask forgiveness for my insensitivity and stupidity.

The descriptions of Buddhist practice and philosophy are accurate as is the dichotomy, if it exists, between Buddhism and other religions.

My purpose in writing this story was to expose certain aspects of Japanese culture not normally evident to or appreciated by an unenlightened community. In addition, I personally felt that such an exposure would help me to sort out the differences I have experienced between my birth religion and Buddhism. I sensed in writing this book a desperate search for a usable ethical method to address and ultimately eradicate, the mountain of ignorance, attachment, and aversion in religious institutions and society. Its purpose consists in the demonstration that there is conflict behind even the most sanctimoniously orthodox, socially unctuous façade.

There is a present gravitation eastwards, which also reflects a prevailing fashion for orientalism that has been growing since the early part of the 20th century. The exotic, mysterious and richly perfumed allure of the East has captivated me.

ACKNOWLEDGEMENT

Nothing is accomplished without help. Firstly, I would like to acknowledge my friend and mentor, Daigaku Rumme who taught me how to experience the Buddhist ethic. Secondly, the monk Taizan Shaeffer who was part of my decision to follow the Henro Pilgrimage and thirdly, Harada Sekkei Roshi, abbot of the Hosshinji Monastery who was my Zen Master and part of my training during the three annual occasions that I attended the Hosshinji Monastery.

I am greatly indebted to my friend Dr. Maurice Siegel who read the manuscript and made many suggestions for change as well as encouraged me to go on during times of ennui. I am grateful for his, encouragement, and good advice that helped shape this book. In addition, I am thankful to Prof. Donald Keene of Columbia University whose body of work, unbeknownst to him, enabled me to grasp the social aspects of Japanese culture.

This book is also lovingly dedicated to my son, Dr. Richard Shansky, who is a walker, hiker and camper and I am sure would appreciate the Henro route.

Finally, to my wife, Pearl Brody Shansky who through patience and presence, while I was away in Japan, encouraged me to fulfill a long time desire to commit to paper my experiences on the Henro Pilgrimage.

I must also give deserved thanks to the Japanese National Tourist Office in Rockefeller Center in New York City for providing me with detailed terrain maps, downloaded from the internet of the Island of Shikoku as well as a comprehensive listing of all 88 Reijo Temples.

EPILOGUE

In the ten years that have transpired between the first trip and the second trip I was busily engaged in visiting and practicing in temples and monasteries in my home area. Among the most memorable was the Zen Mountain Monastery in Mt. Tremper, New York. I also went to The Kagyu Thubten Choling in Wappinger Falls, New York (a Tibetan Buddhist Monastery), and the Tibetan Monastery, Karma Triyana Dharmachakra in Woodstock, New York where I practiced Dzogchen, the Tibetan version of Zazen. And I attended Zen services on Sundays at the Chuang Yen Monastery in Carmel, New York (a Pure Land Chinese Monastery -Jodo Shinshu) where I befriended a female monk named Guna.

In addition, I attended Buddhist courses at the Barre Center for Buddhist Studies in Barre, Massachusetts. I also continued reading Buddhist books on my own as well as many sutras and had worthwhile discussions with Mu Soeng Sunim the Director of the Barre Center. The real breakthrough, so to speak, came in 1992 when I spent several months in the Hosshinji Monastery in Obama, Japan. This took place after the second trip. It was there that I practiced *sesshin* for the first time in June of that year. Sesshin which is a Japanese word and literally means, *collecting the heart mind,* is how I spent a week sitting in intensive zazen (meditation) from 5:30 am to 6:30 pm daily with only short interludes for lunch which is served by the monks at the place where I sat on a platform which surrounds the inner periphery of the zendo.

Zazen is Zen meditation which involves apophatic meditation or emptying the mind of all images. This is distinguished from kataphatic meditation or filling the mind with images. The latter is most prevalent in Tibetan Buddhism. In Zen the idea is to do single-minded sitting (shikantaza) and follow the breath (zuisokkan). When thoughts or images appear one must let them pass through and not to dwell on them. I was given a koan (a conundrum) to solve as part of my training by Harada Sekkei Roshi, the abbot of Hosshinji and my Zen Master, but I was explicitly told not to do koan practice (koan kufu) during zazen. During the twelve hours of sitting, I felt an extreme calmness coming over me despite the arduous nature of the practice every day for a week. After dinner, I was so tired that I crawled into my futon at 9:00pm and fell asleep immediately.

Zen emphasizes the attainment of a sudden enlightenment, or *satori*, through meditation and the freeing of one's own mind from the phenomenal world and from any preconceived notions of reality. I cannot report that I ever became fully enlightened in the Buddhist sense but I did develop a facility for using intuition to a greater degree. In addition, as a result of zazen practice, I am now not as quick to anger and have become more of a critical thinker.

The first state or vehicle, the Shomon, includes those who seek enlightenment for themselves through study and practice. The second state, the Engaku, includes those who gain enlightenment through one's own efforts or realization.

From the moment I arose in the morning at 4:30 am I was aware of the long day ahead of me. I showered, shaved, made up my futon and dressed in a kesa (meditation robe) to appear in the zendo. I located my place on the platform, faced the wall and sat in a half-lotus position. I brought along a shawl which is necessary to ward off the morning cold. By the afternoon the weather turns hot and so I would put the shawl aside until evening. Covered with the shawl I began sitting in the darkened zendo with my eyes half open and my hands folded in my lap. This continues in utter silence for forty minutes. At the conclusion, by a ring of a bell, I arose with the others to walk *kinhin* (walking meditation) in a follow-the-leader style for twenty minutes around the periphery of the zendo. This break was needed because my calves had painful cramps and my right hip bone hurt. The walking is done in a slow rocking motion of first the heal and then the ball of the feet with hands in a gassho position (palms together). This is a reverential moment but also is therapeutic so one can continue in zazen. Then it's back to sitting zazen for another forty minute. This routine is continued over and over again until 6:30 pm.

Meditation is the most important aspect of Buddhist practice and for Zen monk's sesshin of one week or more is usually required. Meditation in Buddhism is the process of training, developing, and purifying the mind, which is likened to an animal which is dangerously destructive when wild, but supremely useful when tamed. It is the third element in the triple training *(trisiksa)* along with conduct or ethics *(sila)* and knowledge or wisdom *(prajna)* and as such is essential to Buddhist practice. There are two aspects, calming the mind *(samatha)* and using the calm mind to see reality clearly *(vipassana)*. These are distinguishable but not distinct. Samatha is attained principally by observing the breathing. It broadly corresponds to meditation. Formless meditation, i.e., holding the mind in the present moment or observing the mind directly is the way of Zen. It is interesting that the triple training is structurally similar to the Benedictine practice of balancing the three elements of liturgy, labor, and study.

In 1981, the date of the first trip to Japan, I had no real definitive knowledge of Buddhism except for the viewing of Buddhist art in museums and observations of Buddhist activity in temples. It was not until the mid-1980s when I attended services at the Minnesota Zen Meditation Center and met Dainin Katagiri Roshi and other of his disciples did I have any insight at all. The trip through the Inland Sea of Japan was my first exposure to Buddhism in action and this piqued my interest for further exploration. This took place during the second trip in 1991. At that time I was only armed with fundamental knowledge but a determination to learn more.

In going through the temples of the Henro Pilgrimage I found that Zen practice has illuminated every aspect of my existence. I learned the key Zen concepts with clarity and simplicity; that was brought to life and resonated with the joy of insight. It was a great and unusual time for me. It was Dainin Katagiri who said, "We often speak of time as though it were a commodity – as something we "save" or "spend" or as something that slips through our fingers before we accomplish what we want. The Zen view is radically, wonderfully different: Time is a creative, dynamic process that continuously produces the universe and everything in it. Understanding this, that there literally is no time to "lose" is the door to freedom." He was one of the most influential teachers of our time and I miss him.

Buddhism is the fourth largest religion in the world with about four hundred million adherents. It ranks in fourth place after Christianity, Islam and Hinduism. The first two religions are growing by proselytizing. The third by population increase in India. Buddhism does not and never have proselytized. Buddhism now exists on all continents except northern Africa, Arctic and Antarctica. Buddhist temples and monasteries exist in North America, Mexico, South America, Europe, Asia and Australia. The growth in all these countries is due to migration of native Chinese, Japanese, Thais, Vietnamese and other Asians to the various countries of the world. In addition, there is an attraction of the native peoples of these countries to Buddhism. Why are so many changing from their birth religions to Buddhism? Can it be that Buddhism offers them something more than their birth religions? How did Buddhism begin and what is it about its philosophy that is so attractive to people schooled in other religions? Let us start at the beginning. Twenty-five hundred years ago in the small Kingdom of Shakya in northern India by the border of western Nepal just south of the present city of Lumbini, in 563 BCE, a birth was taking place in the palace. King Suddhodana awaited impatiently for the birth of his son Siddhartha, the prince. Fabulists have had a field-day with the invention of events in the early life of the prince. The legends which were told about him were mostly unreliable though they may contain a grain of truth here and there. We may believe the following as a minimum. It is said that King Suddhodana, on the advice of an astrologer, kept the prince within the palace grounds for the first eighteen years of his life in order to prevent him from becoming tainted by life in the outside world. Prince Siddhartha Gautama led a cloistered but opulent life inside the palace walls and never ventured outside the palace gates. Then one day out of mostly extraordinary curiosity he opened the palace gates and with his chariot rode into the area beyond the palace walls. He kept riding into the surrounding city. The streets were lined with haggard ghosts, and eyes bulging from hunger stared at him. Siddhartha came across the unmistakable smell of a rotting human corpse. Siddhartha saw that there were other corpses lying about from which came the worst smell. People all about looked angry as they saw his finery. Muttered threats surrounded Siddhartha as he started to leave. An old man stepped forward raising his hands. His starved body was wrapped in dirty hemp cloth. He smelled almost as bad as the corpses. He smiled toothlessly and Siddhartha was ashamed of himself for drawing back. "Young Prince, please help us. There is no food and we are starving to death."

Siddhartha galloped off with the population behind him jeering and catcalling. Others cried out piteously until he reached the palace gates and he could no longer hear them. *I will try to help them. I promise,* he thought. The thought of the poor, starving people who were struck by famine troubled Siddhartha's mind. He could think of nothing else. He sought relief in meditation and prayers to the many gods of Hinduism. He felt no response from them. How could there be such inequity between his life of luxury and the lives of the starving people on the outside? What has caused so much afflictive evil in the world? He decided to seek counsel with the Royal Guru who told him to go into the forest as a mendicant. "This refuge will eventually provide you with wisdom." So one day at the age of twenty-nine Siddhartha gave up family life and became an ascetic. After six years he emerged as the leader of a band of followers who pursued the "middle way" between extreme asceticism and worldly life. He punished his body so much, by giving away his food to the needy, that when he came out of the forest he appeared to be a walking skeleton. He finally reached the city of Ghaya and decided to rest under a sacred papal tree. He fell asleep for some hours but when he awoke a shining light came across his face. He stared into nothingness and he felt a complete state of awareness. He said nothing but his lips moved in unison with his thoughts. "I have the answer," he spoke to himself. One of his followers approached him saying, "Did you speak, Lord?"

He repeated out loud so all could hear, "I have the answer."

"You have the answer to what, Lord?"

"All life is pain and suffering."

"Yes, it is so."

"Pain and suffering is due to desires, grasping and attachments."

"I see."

"The way to eliminate pain and suffering is to eliminate desires, grasping and attachments."

"But how, Lord?"

"The way to eliminate desires, grasping and attachments is to follow a path of carefully disciplined moral conduct culminating in a life of concentration and meditation."

"That is the true doctrine, Lord, but what is the righteous path?"

"It is an eightfold path consisting of right views, right resolve, right speech, right conduct, right livelihood, right effort, right mindfulness, and right concentration. This is the middle way. It is enlightened. It brings clear vision. It makes for wisdom and leads to peace, insight, enlightenment and Nirvana.

Thus the great Dharma common to all Buddhists for over two millennia is the Four Noble Truths and the Eightfold Noble Path. Because of his enlightenment he was henceforth called the Buddha, the awakened one. The Buddha decided to meet with his acolytes in the city of Sarnath where he gave a most important sermon to, a gathering of his followers and others who were interested in a change from Hinduism. After this he spent many years in teaching and organizing his band of followers. He died at about the age of eighty in Kusinara, a small town in the hills. Between the death of the Buddha and the advent of Ashoka, the first great Buddhist emperor, over two hundred years later, there was considerable development of doctrine. Some sort of canon of sacred texts appeared, though it was probable that they were oral. The Buddhists, as a group, acquired numerous lay followers and so Hinduism and Buddhism came to terms as separate disciplines. Buddhists took to settling permanently in monasteries, which were erected on land given by kings and other wealthy patrons.

Quite early in the history of Buddhism sectarian differences appeared. The tradition tells of two great councils of the Buddhist order, the first appeared soon after the Buddha's death, the second a hundred years later. At the latter a schism occurred, and the sect of *Mahasanghikas* (members of the great order) broke away on account of differences on points of monastic discipline and also on doctrinal grounds. The main body, which claimed to maintain the true tradition took to calling their system *Theravada* (the teaching of the Elders). Today this is known as the orthodox sect.

The first great Indian imperial dynasty, the Mauryas, began to rise by land expansion. The third and greatest of the Mauryas, Ashoka, became a Buddhist because he was so moved by remorse at the carnage caused by aggressive war. Buddhism received a great impetus from Ashoka's patronage. It was in Ashoka's reign that Sri Lanka first became a Buddhist country. It has remained a stronghold of the Theravada school since that time. The teaching of the Theravada school is that all things in the universe are composed of; form and matter (*rupa*), sensations (*vedana*), perceptions (*sanna*), psychic dispositions (*samkhara*), and consciousness (vinnana). The individual is made up of these five components. The process of life is explained by Dependent Origination. The root cause of the process of birth and death and rebirth is ignorance, the fundamental illusion that individuality and permanence exist, when in fact they do not. Hence there arise in the organism various psychic phenomena, including desire, followed by an attempt to appropriate things to itself. This concludes with age and death, only to be repeated again and again indefinitely. Rebirth takes place, therefore, according to laws of Karma, which laws do not differ much from Hinduism. The process of rebirth can only be stopped by achieving Nirvana, first by adopting right views about the nature of existence, then by a carefully controlled system of moral conduct and finally by concentration and meditation. These are some of the doctrines of the Theravada school. But the Mahayana sect developed other doctrines. The Theravada sect known as the Hinayana (lesser vehicle) is now prevalent in Sri Lanka, Burma (Myanmar), Thailand, Cambodia, and Laos. The Mahayana (greater vehicle) on the other hand had an idealist world-view. From about the first or second century CE onwards, this new and very different kind of Buddhism arose in India. The new school, which claimed to offer salvation for all, styled itself *Mahayana* (the greater vehicle), as opposed to the older Buddhism, which it contemptuously referred to as *Hinayana*, or (the lesser vehicle). The formula of the three jewels – I take refuge in the Buddha, I take refuge in the *Dharma* (doctrine), I take refuge in the *Sangha* (the order) became the Buddhist profession of faith. A further development was the growth of interest in the *Bodhisattva* (one who delays entry into Nirvana to help others). Passages of Mahayana scriptures describe the self-sacrifice of the Bodhisattva for the welfare of all things living. This is the basic distinction between the old sect and the new. Faith in the Bodhisattvas and the help they afforded was thought to carry many beings along the road to bliss, while the older school which did not accept the Bodhisattva ideal, could save only a few patient and strenuous souls.

The two chief schools of Mahayana philosophy were *Madhyamika* (doctrine of the middle position) and *Yogacara* (the way of the Yoga). The former school taught that the phenomenal world had only a qualified reality. This school was founded by Nagarjuna who lived somewhere between the first and second centuries CE. The Madhyamika philosophers tried to prove that all our experience of the phenomenal world is like laboring under the constant illusion of perceiving things where in fact there is only emptiness. The Yoga-cara School states that the whole universe exists only in the mind of the perceiver. The fact of illusion or the experience of dreams was adduced as evidence to show that all normal human experience was of the same type. Perception therefore is no proof of the independent existence of an entity, and all perceptions may be explained as projections of the percipient mind.

From India Buddhism spread not only to Central Asia and China but also spread to many parts of Southeast Asia. The fourth century CE saw the rise of the second great empire, which at its zenith controlled the whole of northeast India. This was the empire of the Guptas, whose greatest emperors were Hindus. From this period Buddhism began to lose ground in India. Buddhism was beginning to be looked on as a branch of Hinduism, rather than as an independent religion. In the seventh century numerous monasteries, even the sacred Buddhist sites, were deserted and in ruins. The chief stronghold of Buddhism from this time onward was Bihar and Bengal. In Bihar the great Buddhist monastery of Nalanda, founded in the fifth century CE was one of the chief centers of learning in the whole of India. It was from this region that Buddhism was carried in the eighth century to Nepal and Tibet, to be revived and strengthened by later missions in the eleventh century.

At this time, the Hinayana schools had almost disappeared in Eastern India, and allegiance was divided between Mahayana and a new branch referred to as *Vajrayana* (vehicle of the thunderbolt). The Vajrayana crossed the Himalaya Mountains bringing with them *Tantric* views (feminine divinities) and mixing with the indigenous Bon religion of Tibet. There they devoted their chief attention to *Taras* (savioresses). Buddhist monasteries survived in many parts of India until the time of the Muslim invasions at the end of the twelfth century (1192 CE). When the Turkish horsemen occupied Bihar and Bengal they slew or expelled the Buddhist monks and destroyed their monasteries and libraries. Buddhism was, for all intents and purposes, dead in India. Only in the Himalayan regions, especially Nepal, did Buddhism survive, kept alive by contact with Tibet.

When Buddhism came to China, it was spoken of along with the native traditions, Confucianism and Taoism, as one of the Three Teachings or Three Religions, thus achieving a status of virtual equality with these beliefs. While Buddhism was the vehicle for the introduction into such a country as Tibet of religion, art, scripture, literature, philosophy, etc., the Buddhist missionaries found in China a country that possessed these things in an already highly developed state. The movement of Buddhists out of India took a northwesterly turn through present day Afghanistan to the ancient city of Bamiyan where they encountered tradesmen and merchants plying their caravans across the "silk road" into China. These Buddhists remained in Bamiyan for a long time until they completed the rock hewn monumental statues of the Buddha, which were in modern times destroyed by a Muslim group known as the Taliban. These Buddhist missionaries traveled eastward along the Silk Road until they reached Dunhuang in Gansu province where they established the Magao Grottos over a period of several hundred years. However, many continued to penetrate into internal China as far as Luoyang where they completed the Longmen grotto and the Yungong grotto at Datong over another protracted period of time. Buddhism was able to gain a foothold in China because it offered solutions to religious problems which Confucianism did not deal with. Confucianism is of "this world" whereas Buddhism is of the "other world". Taoism departed from the man-centeredness of Confucianism and viewed life in relation to a transcendent, all-pervading way (or Tao) which was the ultimate principal of all life. Thus the Chinese first came into contact with Buddhism through the Buddhist icons worshipped by Central Asians coming into China.

The early Buddhist missionaries brought with them the scriptures containing a precise set of practices. These they believed would enhance the intuitive faculties and are what the Chinese wanted and proceeded to translate. This is the beginning of Buddhist literature in China. A facile interpretation of Buddhism in Neo-Taoist terms prevailed and Buddhism's Indian origins were all but forgotten. The division of Chinese Buddhism into discrete sects had its origins in the tendency to concentrate on the study of one particular scripture or group of scriptures as containing the most essential truths of the religion. Among the great masses of people it was the salvation of the Pure Land sect which prevailed. The schools that have formed the spirit and substance of Chinese Buddhism have been the T'ien-t'ai, Hua-yen, meditation, and Pure Land schools. The meditation school called Ch'an in Chinese from the Sanskrit *dhyana* is best known in the West by the Japanese pronunciation *Zen*. Ch'an is unique in the great emphasis it placed on meditation, using it as a means of attaining an intuitive awareness of the Ultimate Truth. Achievement in meditation was equated with intuitive wisdom. The most commonly used method of bringing a disciple to realization and awakening was that of the *Kung-an* (koan in Japanese). It refers to the enigmatic or paradoxical nature of a brief story or question which has no logical answer but is only used to jolt the mind and formed a planned program of instruction. To defend tradition, however, was the conscious Chinese aim, not to synthesize Confucianism with Buddhism and Taoism. They expressed a belief in the compatibility of the "Three Teachings" (Confucianism, Taoism, and Buddhism).

When Buddhism came to Japan in the sixth century CE, it was young in spirit. Native Shinto, with neither written scriptures nor a formulated theology, could offer resistance only from its entrenched position in the daily lives of the people, but could not compete with Buddhism on its own terms. Buddhism's penetration of Japan, by missionary Korean monks, was facilitated by its identification with the impressive civilization of China. The first historical figure to exemplify the new Buddhist ideal was Prince Shotoku (574-622) regent at the age of twenty-two years, during the reign of his Aunt Empress Suiko. Prince Shotoku received a gift of a Buddha statue and several sutras from the King of Paekche (southern Korea). Under Prince Shotoku's benevolent guidance Buddhist culture flourished in Japan. He was a devout and learned Buddhist, and wrote commentaries on the sacred scriptures of Buddhism. He promoted the construction of monasteries, seminaries, shrines, and chapels. Among these were the monasteries of Horyuji near Nara and Shitennoji in Osaka. A so called constitution of seventeen articles setting forth appropriate rules of public conduct is attributed to him. After Shotoku's time the principle Buddhist sects of the seventh and eighth centuries CE were based on the most advanced teachings of Chinese Buddhism in the period just preceding. The Flower Garland (*Kegon*) school became the closest to becoming the state ideology of the Nara period (eighth century). It preached a cosmic harmony presided over by Lochana Buddha, who sits on a Lotus throne of a thousand petals, each of which is a universe containing thousands of worlds like ours. The entire question of the relationship between the state and Buddhism were most completely discussed in the *Sutra of the Golden Light*. The central theme of the entire sutra is the virtue of wisdom – *prajna*, which distinguishes good from evil and right from wrong.

The monk Saicho (767-822) and the temple he founded on Mt. Hiei were to develop into the center of learning and culture of the entire nation. Saicho was sent to China in 804, chiefly to gain spiritual sanction for the new Buddhist foundation on Mt. Hiei. While he was in China he studied the Tendai (T'ien-t'ai) teachings, and he brought back this doctrine to Japan after a year abroad. The Tendai sect was based on the teachings of the *Lotus Sutra*, which states that in every person, is the Buddha-nature and no matter how wicked a man may be, he is potentially a Buddha.

A threat to the prosperity of Tendai came in the return to Japan of Kukai (774-835) who was to become the great religious leader of the period. Kukai's Shingon (true words) Buddhism with its emphasis on aestheticism, was higher in favor with the court than the severely moral Tendai School. In 816 he built a monastery on Mt. Koya which later became the center of the Shingon sect. In 822 Saicho, Kukai's rival died and in the following year Kukai was appointed Abbot of the Toji, the great Buddhist temple which commanded the main entrance to the capital. He died in 835 on Mt. Koya and was given the honorific title, Kobo Daishi (Kobo, great teacher). Kukai established a series of 88 temples around the periphery of the island of Shikoku. This became a pilgrimage called the Henro. It takes about two months to walk from temple number one to temple number eighty-eight. It, of course, is still in use today and is described by the author in the second trip of this book.

In the twelfth century no Buddhist doctrine or sect was more influential than that associated with the Buddha Amida whose Western Paradise or "Pure Land" offered a haven to weary souls in the strife-torn age. It was Amida, the Buddha of Boundless Light, who eons ago vowed that all should be saved who called his name, *Namu Amida Butsu* (Hail Amida Buddha), with single-minded and whole hearted devotion. This was the invocation which became known as the *Nembutsu*, a term which originally signified meditation on the name of Amida. The spread of Pure Land doctrines in medieval times represented a striking change in outlook for the Japanese. With the appearance of Honen (1133-1212) a sharp break with other forms of Buddhism occurred. At the age of seventy-four Honen's success in winning converts to the new Pure Land sect, which he had founded and known as *Jodoshu*, resulted in his condemnation and exile. Among those banished from Kyoto at the same time as Honen was Shinran (1173-1262), who was the true disciple of Honen and is regarded as the founder of the most important of all Pure Land sects, the *Jodo Shinshu*, (the true Jodoshu). Shinran's crime, for which he was exiled to the northern province of Echigo, was that he had taken a wife in violation of the clerical vow of celibacy. Her name was Eshinni. Letters she wrote while in Echigo tell the true story of their marriage and their faith in the Jodo Shinshu sect. Their grandson started the Hongwanji movement which is presently active in Japan and some major cities in the United States.

Nichiren (1222-1282) the son of a humble fisherman spent years in study and training at the great monastic center of Mt. Hiei. He embarked on a preaching career of unceasing hardship, conflict, and persecution. For Nichiren the *Lotus Sutra*, upon which the Tendai teaching had been based, is the key to everything. Like Shinran, Nichiren was a man of no slight intelligence, and in his years of exile or enforced seclusion he devoted himself to an intensive study of scripture and doctrine; but this erudition only served to adorn a simple conviction, arrived at early in life and held to with single-minded devotion throughout his stormy career, that faith in the *Lotus of the Wonderful Law* was all one needed for salvation.

The immediate cause of his suffering was Nichiren's unrelenting attack on the established sects and his outspoken criticism of Japan's rulers for patronizing these heretics. The Pure Land and Nichiren sects stressed the need for complete faith in something beyond oneself; the saving power of Amida or of the Lotus sutra, to find rest and security, they said, man had to turn from himself and this world to the Other World.

By contrast Zen Buddhism, which first rose to prominence in these same times, firmly opposed the idea that Buddhahood is something to be sought outside oneself or in another world. Every man has a Buddha-nature, and to realize it he need only look within. Self-understanding and self-reliance are the keynote of Zen. Ch'an missionaries often accompanied trading missions to Japan. It is understandable, then, why Ch'an Buddhism should have deeply implanted itself on Japanese soil at this time, during the twelfth and thirteenth centuries. Two great Japanese pioneers of Zen established this teaching firmly on native ground. These pioneers were Eisai (1141-1215) and Dogen (1200-1253). Zen is much more than a single enlightenment experience; it is a whole way of life. We are fortunate that in the biographies of these two Zen pioneers we have a much fuller account of their activities, providing us with the important links between Zen as they saw it, Zen as they lived it, and Zen as it had an impact on many aspects of Japanese life and culture.

In twelfth century China Eisai found Zen to be the only form of Buddhism still flourishing, and after studying at the Zen center of *T'ien-t'ung shan*, returned to Japan in 1191 as a full-fledged Zen master of the Rinzai (in Chinese, *Lin-chi*) school. The major, and possibly, only difference between Rinzai Zen and other forms such as Soto Zen is their unrelenting reliance on koan solving, leading to the attainment of sudden enlightenment. At the historic centers of Buddhist monasticism, Mt. Hiei and Miidera near Lake Biwa, Dogen was disappointed to find no true refuge from worldly life and only an academic or ritualistic interest in the Buddhist ideal. Dogen's attitude toward traditional Buddhism was notably softer than most of his Zen predecessors in China. The study of scripture was not to be condemned, except where it led to the sutras' gaining mastery over the student rather than the student gaining mastery over the sutras. From the point of view of Dogen, and the Soto (Chinese *tsao-tung*) school of Zen which he introduced to Japan, this preoccupation with momentary experience of enlightenment and the deliberate use of the koan formula to achieve it was directed too much toward obtaining a certain thing and might be too self-assertive. It also placed too great stress on mental perception, realization through the mind alone rather than through all the faculties and activities of the whole man. Therefore Dogen minimized the value of the koan and stressed instead the importance of sitting in meditation (*zazen*) without any thought of acquisition or attainment, without any specific problem in mind. Dogen established the Eiheiji Monastery in Fukui, Japan. It is presently the headquarter monastery of a number of monasteries in Japan and other parts of the world. He also authored the Shobogenzo which is considered almost as a bible for Soto Zen.

Hakuin (1686-1769) is the father of modern Rinzai Zen; all present-day masters of this sect claim descent from him. He was an extraordinary man, indomitable in his search for the truth of Zen. He gave all his efforts to the revival of Zen Buddhism. He rejected formalistic and intellectual Zen, as well as the syncretism with the Nembutsu practice which was popular in China at the time. Denouncing all secular ambitions among the clergy, he dedicated himself to the promotion of what he considered true Zen. Today there are about fifteen million Zen Buddhists in Japan. Up to about World War II there has been a steady migration of Buddhism of various sects throughout the world to lodge itself in juxtaposition with other religions. After the Second World War, Buddhism became of interest to the western world. Soldiers returning from Asia as well as certain intellectuals and religious clergy brought with them some of the Buddhist teachings they encountered amongst Asian people. In the 1960s the "beat generation" in the United States as well as Canada and Europe became interested in Buddhism as a way of overcoming conventional traditions to the point of traveling to various countries in Asia to learn and practice more. Today, in the United States the most popular sects of Buddhism are Tibetan, Zen, Pure Land, Vipassana and Nichiren. These sects, with their hierarchies, have their own temples and monasteries where they practice an American version of Buddhism. Buddhism is exponentially growing in almost all western countries and even the universities have introduced curricula of Eastern religion and philosophy.

3993797

Made in the USA
Lexington, KY
14 December 2009